Stumbling Toward
OBEDIENCE

*Learning from Jonah's Failure to Love God
and the People He Came to Save*

DAVID R. HAWKINS

WestBow
PRESS
A DIVISION OF THOMAS NELSON

Copyright © 2013 David R. Hawkins.

All rights reserved. No part of this book may be used or reproduced by any means, graphic, electronic, or mechanical, including photocopying, recording, taping or by any information storage retrieval system without the written permission of the publisher except in the case of brief quotations embodied in critical articles and reviews.

WestBow Press books may be ordered through booksellers or by contacting:

WestBow Press
A Division of Thomas Nelson
1663 Liberty Drive
Bloomington, IN 47403
www.westbowpress.com
1-(866) 928-1240

Because of the dynamic nature of the Internet, any web addresses or links contained in this book may have changed since publication and may no longer be valid. The views expressed in this work are solely those of the author and do not necessarily reflect the views of the publisher, and the publisher hereby disclaims any responsibility for them.

Any people depicted in stock imagery provided by Thinkstock are models, and such images are being used for illustrative purposes only. Certain stock imagery © Thinkstock.

Scripture taken from the New King James Version®. Copyright © 1982 by Thomas Nelson, Inc. Used by permission. All rights reserved.

ISBN: 978-1-4497-9907-6 (sc)
ISBN: 978-1-4497-9908-3 (hc)
ISBN: 978-1-4497-9906-9 (e)

Library of Congress Control Number: 2013911355

Printed in the United States of America.

WestBow Press rev. date: 07/01/2013

Dedication

*To my beloved Vickie,
my wife and companion of thirty-nine years, and
God's most precious gift to me in life.*

*Her heart for God is deeper and more surrendered
than anyone I have ever known.
Her deep musings on the Word of God
and her exemplary pursuit of God
help spur me on toward uncompromising obedience
on the straight and narrow way.*

Special thanks is offered to Bethany Goccia, our second daughter, whose natural abilities with words has always amazed as well as entertained us. Also Sam Whicker, our first son-in-law, fellow pastor, and beloved member of our family. Both of these family members served me by reading, editing, kindly offering their suggestions, and by simply putting forth their loving efforts to help. Their kind suggestions helped take me from wordy clutter to a more down-to-earth approach. Thank you.

These family members (and all our family which now numbers 15) are so precious to us as fellow redeemed sinners and pilgrims in the grace of Jesus.

You all are so loved!

Table of Contents

Introduction xi

PART 1 **God's Call Upon Every Servant**
Jonah 1:1-2

Chapter 1 Under Orders 3

PART 2 **The Anatomy of Stumbling**
Jonah 1:1 - 16

Chapter 2 God Speaks, But We Choose a Different Pathway 11

Chapter 3 Sleeping While Others Are Perishing 25

Chapter 4 Giving Lip-Service to Following God in the Midst of Rebellion 31

Chapter 5 Choosing Death Over Repentance 35

PART 3 **God's Discipline and the Servant's Restoration**
Jonah 1:17 - 4:11

Chapter 6 Swallowed Up in God's Discipline 41

Chapter 7 The God of the Second Chance 57

Chapter 8	The God Who Pursues Sinners	71
Chapter 9	The Sins of a Stumbling Heart	79
Chapter 10	Ensuring Obedience has a Fighting Chance	95
	A Final Word	107

Introduction

Why would I write about stumbling? Frankly, I have a lot of experience. Ultimately, we want to examine the state of our hearts that leads us to stumbling so that we may achieve a more consistent obedience to our Lord. Scripture's command is that we "Walk in a manner worthy of the calling with which you were called" (Ephesians 4:1). But in my walk with God, I have at times frustrated myself when I kept retaking the same ground over and over. It is as though whatever steps forward I took, I then fell backward several steps.

The Bible says in James 3:2, "We all stumble in many ways." And as I engage self-evaluation, I have to ask myself: Why do I fail the Lord? Why do I so often pursue my own agenda, while laying claim to being *His* servant and clinging to *His* agenda? How can I in one moment exult in who Christ is and that I am forever His, and then shortly afterward have attitudes and thoughts that are anything but Christlike?

None of us likes to admit it, but hearts that stumble are something we all wrestle with. As Christians, we intensely dislike this heart tendency of ours. But victory is first achieved by understanding something about the nature of our hearts, even as God's redeemed ones. Jeremiah 17:9 provides a startlingly direct revelation of what our hearts are truly like: "The heart is deceitful above all things, and desperately wicked; who can know it?" Truly, when it comes to the state of our natural hearts, the news is not good.

Although in Christ our hearts have been made new, subtle intrusions can enter in that often go unnoticed or uncorrected. Thus, a once passionate and vital walk with God can gradually, even stealthily, become unresponsive and hardened. While we ought to remain tender and pliable toward God, the sad reality is that we don't always.

In the wilderness, Israel experienced a hardening when they refused to act in faith to receive the promises of God concerning a new land. King Solomon, although beginning well and being greatly blessed by God, eventually allowed his heart to be turned away from a pure devotion to God. Eclipsed by lesser loves, Solomon's heart became calloused where once it was sensitive. In the New Testament, Ananias and Sapphira experienced the same. All these examples had tragically similar endings, as is most often the case with hearts that stumble.

Someone once said that the same sun that melts the butter also hardens the clay. The difference, of course, is in the nature of the object affected by the sun's heat. Similarly, the genuine child of God ought to be one that melts into pliability in God's hands, rather than turn from usefulness into hardened clay that is no longer fit for His service. We are warned in Hebrews 3:8 to keep a vigilant posture toward the tendency of our own hearts. Written to genuine believers in Jesus Christ, the author of Hebrews says: "Harden not your hearts, as in the provocation, in the day of temptation in the wilderness." Notice that the responsibility to avert a hardening of the heart is on the individual believer.

In his hymn, "Come, Thou Fount of Every Blessing," Robert Robinson wrote of his own heart's tendency toward stumbling:

"Prone to wander, Lord, I feel it; Prone to leave the God I love." After penning these words, he eventually wandered away from God, becoming a faith casualty. This sad commentary is not reserved for Mr. Robinson alone. It can happen to any of God's servants in any life setting. If we are not constantly vigilant toward that which would quench the fire of God in our hearts, the passion for Him will soon die as a result of the hardening toward His ways. Gail MacDonald put it poignantly in her book, *High Call, High Privilege,* "Untended fires soon die and become a pile of ashes." This is why we must constantly exercise ourselves toward vigilance concerning that which would douse the fires of our heart's passion for God. The cry of our hearts must ever and always be: "O make me Thine forever, and should I fainting be, Lord, let me never, never, outlive my love to Thee."[1]

Repeatedly God has drawn my attention to the prophet Jonah. Honestly, though, when I first began studying Jonah, I did so with disobedient believers in mind – people who (in my experience) had wandered from God, substituting their own life pursuits for fulfilling His will. But the more I have walked through a few sovereignly orchestrated events of life, I've been humbled to see more of what *I'm* truly made of. I have realized that Jonah's life is not so far removed from the tendencies of my own heart. And because 1 Corinthians 10:13 teaches us that all temptation is common, I have confidence that what God is saying to me, He also wants to say to you. So this book (in the words I once heard) is one beggar showing other beggars where to find bread.

The lessons from Jonah's life may prevent us from growing hardhearted and stumbling to the point of ultimate failure in our service to our Lord. Avoiding a fatal stumbling, however, requires that we take heed. The lessons from Jonah's heart and life may even soften some hearts that have already set out on the pathway

---

[1] Hymn, *O Sacred Head, Now Wounded.* Public Domain

to becoming unresponsive and calloused toward God—the precursors to spiritual failure.

I have assumptions as I write. First, that you may have picked up this book out of a personal identification with its title, for we all struggle with our flesh and its warfare against the Spirit. We are all in the same boat; we are all made of the same human "fabric" with all its sinful tendencies. Secondly, I assume that men and women of God are still men and women—sinners in need of God's sanctifying grace in our daily lives. We still fail God and at times do so in great measure and with huge consequences. Thirdly, even saved and redeemed people occasionally need help to master their sinful bent. That is where Jonah will help us immeasurably. And the deeper we immerse ourselves in his book (his Spirit-inspired written testimony), the more deeply and completely we may come to understand our own hearts.

With these assumptions in mind and the study of Jonah's stumbling in front of us, we must guard ourselves from a *this could never happen to me* attitude. 1 Corinthians 10:12 exhorts us, "Let him who thinks he stands take heed lest he fall." Said another way, if we think it couldn't happen to us, then we are prime candidates for failure. Therefore, the humility of walking with Jesus must include a perpetual caution toward our heart's tendency to stray. With this in view, learning and embracing these lessons is essential—lessons that come directly from Jonah's own testimony concerning his call, his disobedience, and his return to obedience.

I am not a psychologist; I am a pastor and a missionary by calling and by profession. By the Spirit's gifting, I am a shepherd of God's people. Therefore, it is my concern for the spiritual health of God's people that drives me to write this book. I believe unequivocally in the power of God to change lives. I think there is a place for therapy and counseling, but the core of who we are as believers in Jesus Christ is a matter of the condition and the maintenance of our hearts. God created our hearts, and the divine "therapy" of His Word is His primary and sufficient means for dealing with our prone-to-wander hearts.

My purpose in this book is to deal with *the fact* of a stumbling heart and its *evidences*. In doing so, we will touch on the *why* of stumbling (as far as Jonah's book allows). There are many wonderful resources for unraveling what has led to a failure in the heart of a servant of God and it is not my purpose here to duplicate those works. But as we learn how our hearts can become calloused, we must also learn how to choose behaviors that will avoid such slippery slopes. These lessons will become apparent as we progress in our study. Furthermore, it is my built-in premise that the revelation of a sin issue is also the invitation of God to confess it, forsake it, and enjoy afresh the relationship with God into which He has called us.

Romans 15:4 says, "the things that were written before were written for our learning, that we through patience and encouragement of the Scriptures might have hope." This New Testament promise surely includes Jonah's Old Testament book. So as we learn from the prophet Jonah and his experiences that have preceded ours, it is my hope that God will have a purer, more passionate servant for His use, and one more honest at the heart level. May God be glorified as we study His Word and become changed for His glory.

PART 1

*God's Call Upon
Every Servant*

Jonah 1:1-2

1
Under Orders

> Now the word of the Lord came to Jonah ...
> "Arise and go to Nineveh."
>
> —Jonah 1:1–2

Fix bayonets! The order rang out at the top of his voice, clear and urgent, above the din of battle. With half of his men either dead or wounded and facing another impending Confederate advance, Colonel Joshua Lawrence Chamberlain's men were in desperate straits. Tasked to defend a hill on the extreme left of the Union line at Gettysburg and nearly out of ammunition, the colonel had little choice but to order a bayonet charge against the advancing Confederates. It was not a time for a roundtable discussion of strategies or options. The enemy was visibly on the move, and a decision had to be made. Chamberlain's men obeyed his command (some of them at the cost of their own lives) and held the hill. This event helped turn the battle of Gettysburg into a Union victory, a victory that would become the turning point for the War between the States and ultimately lead to a reunited United States.

Why did Colonel Chamberlain's men, with only bayonets, follow this seemingly insane order to charge down a hill toward an armed enemy? Some would say they had no other choice, because they were military men. While it is true they were obligated to obey their commander's orders, the reasons go much deeper. Colonel Chamberlain had demonstrated the kind of leadership that makes a commander beloved. Thus, he was a trusted leader, and in the situation his regiment faced on Little Round Top in July of 1863, his command was followed without question.

Military personnel understand orders. They are given so the group will adhere and conform to an expectation that has come from higher up the command structure. Consequences of disobedience may be dire, even fatal. Everyone understands orders exist even if only some of us adhere to them well. And whether it is in the context of employer, parent, or military service, when an order is given (assuming it is proper and legal), it is meant to be obeyed.

God is far more than a beloved and trusted commanding officer. He is the One of whom none is greater, existing unrivaled as the supreme and sovereign authority over all that is. But more than that, He is the author of our salvation, a beloved heavenly Father, who has sent His only Son as our substitute to bear our punishment for sin. His supreme gift of His Son brought to sinners eternal redemption and life and fellowship with Himself. So because of who He is and what He has done for His people, when God says to do something, that something ought to be done. Like their Lord, all followers of God ought to be about their Father's business. No one is exempt from obedience to God's revealed will.

We ought to obey God simply because He gave a command. "Because I said so," in some circumstances, can be a poor reason given to children for obedience, but not when God is the father and we are the children. Human parents use these words when frustrated with little mouths offering their opinions or resistance—both of which are unwelcome in the face of a parental command. But *because He said so* is an entirely appropriate reason for a Christian to consistently choose obedience to God. It is His Word, recorded for us as the Bible, by which we all will be held accountable. Second Corinthians 5:10 reveals these sobering words: "For we must all appear before the judgment seat of Christ, that each one may receive the things done in the body, according to what he has done, whether good or bad." *Bad* in the original language can also be understood as "empty" or "vain." Our actions, as well-meaning and socially profitable as they may be, are empty and vain when they are in disharmony with God's agenda and His commands.

Additionally, the teachings of Jesus about the agenda of His kingdom on earth are the very words that will be the template of our accountability. In Revelation 1 we see a vision of heaven with the exalted Christ and out of His mouth comes a two-edged sword (see verse 16). This sword is His Word. His Word is His command, and His commands always come from His heart for the good of His children and the glory of His name. As God's children, in relationship with Him through Jesus Christ, we bear the responsibility to obey the Word of our Father. Whether or not we obey our Father—engaging His agenda—will most certainly be the point of accountability on the day of reckoning.

Before ascending back into the glorious presence from which He came, Jesus gave the Great Commission to His disciples (Matthew 29:19), that "Going," we were to "make disciples of all peoples." His words are plain and to the point: God's heart is to save lost people. The Scriptures affirm, "[F]or He is not willing that any should perish."[2] Disciple-making begins with proclaiming the truth of the gospel to those around us who are lost—still

---

[2] Second Peter 3:9.

outside a redemptive relationship with their Creator and the Lord Jesus Christ, who gave Himself on their behalf. It continues with helping them learn to embrace His ways in lifestyles of consistent obedience and to become spiritual reproducers themselves.

Jesus lived on the same planet that we do. He experienced all the hassles of life, the myriad temptations, the daily pressures, and the stresses of family life, work, and society. And as a man, experiencing everything that people experience (see Hebrews 4:15), He demonstrated *complete* submission to the Father's will to the point of His confident assertion, "I always do those things that please My Father" (John 8:29). He gave Himself in humility at Calvary to satisfy God's wrath against all sin, as well as all sinners, and declared from the cross, "It is finished." What was finished? The divinely judicial satisfaction that all sin, for all humankind, for all time was paid for by His sacrifice on Calvary's cross. He then experienced death but rose in victory over death, thus proving His claims to divinity and giving to all His spiritual descendants resurrection power for daily living.

So what is to be our response to all Christ Jesus is and all that He has suffered and accomplished on our behalf? What should be our life's focus, our objective, our agenda, and our passion? Obedience to the things our Lord and Savior has commanded. Obedience is our duty, to be sure, but it is more than that. It is the way we express our thanksgiving for what Christ has done for us. It is gratefulness lived out on a daily basis. This kind of living involves a consistent orientation toward laying aside personal or selfish desires and agendas that bring us temporal gratification. Instead, we embrace what Jesus Christ tells us to do: to proclaim the gospel of hope to those who know it not. This is the highest expression of gratefulness from a life made new by the living Lord.

Obedience to the Great Commission is still God's expectation for His people. The command is clear, and God has exempted no one from its authority. The proclamation of the gospel message from one person to another is the divine call placed upon every servant of Jesus Christ, professional or layperson. Far excelling social change, political action, or behavioral modification (all of which may have their place), obedience to the Great Commission is the way the kingdom of God comes, changing individuals, families, neighborhoods, societies, cultures, and nations through the power of the gospel of Jesus Christ.

One of the most dismal realities in modern Christendom is the amazing lethargy in the church toward the Great Commission of our Lord Jesus Christ. It is a sad state of normalcy that the church today exists often mainly for itself—its agenda, its programs, its budget, its reputation and ability to draw a crowd, and many other things of a temporal nature. The study of Jonah's stumbling is written with a deep disturbance at what I observe in the modern church. The church of our day is satisfied to bask in the benefits of knowing God, but it has grown calloused and cold toward actually doing what He says. Rarely do we hear the testimony of the newly saved in church anymore. How infrequently do confessing Christians converse with a mutual desire to help one another in their pursuit of obedience to God's call? Much like the prophet who got on the ship to Tarshish, the church has departed from God's presence. The only difference is that Jonah admitted he was fleeing from God. The modern church, on the other hand, operates under the misguided assumption that its democratic way of doing business, entertainment-oriented worship services, and myriad programs aimed at attracting the masses are, in fact, living in God's presence. Yet, all the while—and like Jonah—the presence of God may very well have been left far behind.

I do not have the ability to unravel all of why Christians do not engage the Lord's commands, but as far as Jonah's story will allow, we will examine what it is like to stumble toward an obedience we all know should be normal—a *biblically* normal obedience.

Obedience to Christ's commission, engaging the lost in clear and intentional dialogue concerning their need for the Savior, ought to be the norm for the life of one made new by a redemptive relationship with Jesus Christ. Charles Spurgeon underscores this premise with such power and beauty: "I will not believe that thou has tasted of the honey of the gospel if thou canst eat it all thyself. True grace puts an end to all spiritual monopoly."[3]

Evangelism as we go through this life is the outworking of the normal life of grace. And the evangelistic call has come down to us from the King above all kings. His authority is over all, especially His household of redeemed people who have embraced His salvation. And regarding His call to obey His Great Commission, there are no exceptions. No one is excluded, and there are no valid excuses for disobedience. God's commands are given so God's agenda for the kingdom of Christ will be fulfilled. These statements are not made in order to be harsh but to be truthful. Ignoring them or pretending our disobedience will somehow be divinely winked at someday is utter foolishness. We must recognize the calling that is upon us and our failure to engage it. Then we must do something about what we know.

It is the mark of every genuine child of God that he sincerely desires to live in consistent obedience, but he also stumbles in many ways and on many fronts. Jonah's testimony will greatly help all who sincerely desire to cling tightly to Christ and His commands. "If anyone loves Me he will keep My word." These are the words of our Lord Jesus (John 14:23). This is what every true Christian wants, so let's press on into Jonah's writing and learn how we may stumble less and obey our Lord and Savior more.

---

[3] Charles H. Spurgeon, *Morning and Evening*, February 19. Hendrickson Publishers.

PART 2

The Anatomy of Stumbling

Jonah 1:1 - 16

2
God Speaks, But We Choose a Different Pathway

> Now the word of the Lord came to Jonah...
> But Jonah arose to flee to Tarshish from
> the presence of the Lord.
>
> —Jonah 1:1-3

Why do Christians read and understand Christ's teachings, but allow the priority of obeying them to fade from view? Why do we not engage the responsibility our Lord Jesus Christ has placed upon us? The short answer is because we have *chosen* other priorities. We pursue lesser objectives (things of a temporal nature), inadvertently acquiescing to these as our life's purpose and that which would bring us fulfillment. Like Jonah, God has spoken and we have heard, but *we* have chosen to go in a different direction.

People who claim to be Christian people, yet have substituted God's commands for something less, have in fact inverted their life's values. What ought to be a daily joyful adherence to God's agenda for life is slowly lost in the pursuit of other things—things of an earthly, temporal nature. A person who has inverted his values does not easily perceive what he is truly like, the upside-down manner in which he lives. Such a person may live outwardly like everything is in its spiritual place—church attendance, saying the right things when in the presence of other church people, praying before meals, giving, etc.—but rarely (if ever) does he think in terms of evaluating his life by the standard of normalcy as revealed in the Bible. He almost never seeks opportunities to proclaim the gospel to the lost, not even the lost in his immediate context. Oh, he may give money (perhaps even sacrificially) so that *missionaries* can tell others of Jesus in that faraway land, but will he tell his co-workers, his family members, or his neighbors of Christ's grace—those people who speak his language, who are within walking distance, or those with whom he could go to lunch anytime and engage in conversation over spiritual matters?

Living a life with inverted values does not happen suddenly. As a Christian, you don't one day wake up and say, "Today I'm going to forget everything I know about my relationship with God and do things my way." No, it doesn't happen that way to a true believer. It begins by small compromises in the heart, like a small cloud that blocks out the sun's brightness for a short time. After repeated compromises, the clouds continue gathering to the point of a completely overcast conscience, blocking the brightness of the Spirit's presence and His prompting. Repeated compromises eventually harden the heart of one who once followed passionately after God.

Choices and Their Consequences

We can't see what's inside a person, so how do we recognize when a person's heart (or our own heart) is leaving God's values for lesser ones? Proverbs 4:23 teaches us about behavior and where it comes from, "Keep your heart with all diligence, for out of it spring the issues of life." Simply said, the manner in which we behave flows out of who we are at the core of our being – what we commonly refer to as *the heart*. Said another way, we face life through the grid of who we are on the inside, what we call our *thinking*. Our thought process is the manifestation of our innermost being and is molded from our youth upward by our circumstances and, more significantly, by our responses to those circumstances.

Maintaining that core being in a posture of responsiveness to God is absolutely essential and is the message of so much of Scripture as well as the message of this book. Life comes complete with hard times, difficult people, and circumstances that can surprise us as much as being jolted by a sudden sound in the night. Things happen, wounds come, problems arise and responses of the heart are not always in harmony with what the Spirit of God would have us do. Wrong responses come from wrong choices, and those choices have consequences. They begin a process of hardening in the heart that is as multifaceted as it is treacherous.

I am reminded of a sermon I once observed. The speaker was illustrating this very point and held a full glass of water in his hand. As he taught on the subject of maintaining the heart, he began to shake the glass roughly and water sloshed out everywhere. He paused and asked the congregation, "Why did water splash out of the glass?" "Because you shook it," some answered, but with a sly smile he corrected them saying, "No, water came out of the glass because water was inside the glass. Likewise, whatever is inside our hearts will also splash out when life's adversities begin to shake us." This poignant sermon illustration became a defining moment of comprehension for me, because it brought to the forefront of my mind how desperately I must seek to keep my heart responsive to God and pliable in His hands.

Peering into Jonah's Inverted Priorities

What are the signs that a heart is beginning to grow calloused toward God or His ways, indications that we are losing God's priorities for life and substituting lesser ones in their place? Jonah's book is his personal testimony. It is his own account of his wayward heart and its resulting aberrant behavior. The book itself suggests that it was written sometime after his ordeal, and as such, his post-rebellion reflection provides a rather stimulating perspective as well as some definite answers for the disciple who is desirous of genuine holiness and growth toward the image of Christ.

Jonah was a prophet of Yahweh. He was called, equipped, and experienced in listening to God and speaking His Words. But there is something else about Jonah that is most apparent from his book; he was very stubborn. Like a spoiled child, he had his own ideas of what an obedient life was to look like in terms of its demands on him and the level of inconvenience it might invoke. Jonah's paradigm for his obedience had human limits to it and it certainly *did not* include those ungodly Ninevites.

Think of the incredible contradiction within the heart of God's servant. His calling was to proclaim the way of salvation to people totally ignorant of that way and desperately in need of it. They were facing the threat of divine destruction because of their sin and Jonah knew this well. Yet he resisted telling them, even rejected them as possible recipients of God's mercies. As a result of his heart's failure to adhere to God's heart for lost people and after hearing God's clear command, without uttering a word he simply got on a ship going exactly the opposite direction from where he should have been going.

Jonah disobeyed God, but his problem was far worse than that. His heart had grown indifferent toward God's heart for His world.

God spoke clearly to him, "Go to Nineveh…and cry out against it; for their wickedness has come up before Me."[4] This is our God, whose heart is that lost people—people who are outside of a saving relationship with Him—hear the truth, repent, and come into a genuine, saving relationship with Him. Jonah disregarded God's call and demonstrated that his heart was stumbling in its obedience. God gave a clear word, and he chose a different direction. We do this same thing when our values become inverted and different from God's.

Jonah's Credentials

Why did Jonah not obey God? Did he not hear Him? Did he somehow misunderstand what God said? None of these scenarios is likely. Jonah was accustomed to hearing God's voice. He was a notable prophet. He prophesied by profession and most likely lived during the 8th century BC, a day of prosperity for the northern kingdom of Israel. That season in Israel's history saw their national borders extended under the military campaigns of Jeroboam II. Second Kings 14:25 speaks of the northern kingdom of Israel and its successes in Jonah's day,

> [King Jeroboam II] restored the coast of Israel from the entrance of Hamath unto the sea of the plain, according to the word of the LORD God of Israel, which *He spoke by the hand of his servant Jonah, the son of Amittai, the prophet, which was of Gath Hepher.* (emphasis mine)

So clearly, hearing God's voice was no once-in-a-while occurrence to Jonah. He did not mistake what he heard for something other than God's voice. He was what we might call a professional "man of God" – the *clergy* of his day. Being the spokesman for God was his job, his profession. It was his calling and one in which he had

---
[4] Jonah 1:2

ample experience. Yet in the face of this clear word from God to go to Nineveh, Jonah's darkening, stumbling heart became manifest. He chose a different pathway – the pathway of disobedience, of human logic and rationale, of his own agenda (for reasons that will become clear later in our study). God spoke, and Jonah ran in the opposite direction.

Being a professional man of God doesn't in itself produce a love for God's priorities. Someone who isn't embracing God's heart for His world will not suddenly begin to do so if he becomes a preacher or a missionary. Knowing what to do and being paid to do it do not always equal an obedient follower of God. Neither does possessing a clear and articulated knowledge of God's will necessitate a passionate adherence to that will in the heart. Any of God's people, from the most influential and esteemed down to the lowliest, can allow lesser emphases to slowly eclipse their love for Jesus that once occupied the place of preeminence in their hearts, that one encompassed their entire lives.

Overcoming Inverted Priorities

Revelation 12:11 speaks of the holiest of passions for obedience to God's redemptive plan this way, "And they overcame him by the blood of the Lamb and by the word of their testimony, and they did not love their lives to the death." Overcoming is what obedience is all about—overcoming the world's lure, overcoming the flesh and its lusts, overcoming the devil himself and all he throws in front of us to distract and destroy our relationships (and thus our testimonies) with God. This group of saints in Revelation overcame by the blood of the Lamb (by being in Christ, loving Him above all), and by the word of their testimony (by choosing to identify with Christ in this world, speaking to the lost concerning the free pardon from sin's curse through Jesus Christ). It was that simple. They understood who they were in Christ and they spoke about the reality of their relationship with Christ and how others could know Him as well. Sharing the gospel is not complicated or mysterious. It is simply telling people how they might be saved from the divine wrath that is upon the human race because of sin.

How passionate for this gospel were the saints spoken of in Revelation 12? *They did not love their lives to the death.* Obedience meant more to them than their own lives. Undeniably, self-preservation is a powerful human instinct, but in the face of a choice between obeying Christ's commission to proclaim to those who needed to be saved or to save their own necks, they chose to obey Christ, leaving the fate of *their own* lives in the hands of the sovereign, providential Lord whom they trusted and served with zeal and passion.

God's calling is that we, first and foremost, love the Lord our God. Jesus' own words were that loving the Lord is the first and greatest commandment. Nothing is more important.

> "'You shall love the Lord your God with all your heart, with all your soul, and with all your mind.' This is the first and great commandment. And the second is like it: 'You shall love your neighbor as yourself. *On these two commandments hang all the Law and the Prophets.*"[5] (emphasis mine)

The relationship God has provided for every genuine believer in Jesus Christ is the most important and most compelling relationship known to mankind. And truly loving God means that we also love what He loves—people. Not just people who are like us, who are in our socio-economic bracket, or who are easy to love, but all people, and especially those outside of a saving relationship with God. It is a constant battle to keep

---

[5] Matthew 22:37-40

worldly philosophies and passions from tantalizing our hearts and causing us to drift away from our first love of devotion to Jesus.

Biblical Priorities

Pausing for a few minutes to examine our own lives in light of our biblical calling is appropriate here. Are we, like Jonah, susceptible to a drifting of the heart away from its first priority of passion for God and His ways? Let's look at a few of God's commands to us, clearly articulated to New Testament believers, that we might not be acting upon in full obedience.

Scripture makes very clear what our calling as the people of God ought to be like as it is lived out in the world. 1 Corinthians 6:20 instructs us: "For you were bought with a price: therefore glorify God in your body, and in your spirit, which are God's." Colossians 3:17 gives us a similar instruction: "And whatever you do in word or deed, do all in the name of the Lord Jesus, giving thanks to God the Father through Him."

To operate in Christ's name is for Christ alone to receive the attention (the credit, the glory) for what is done. One of the main elements of the believer's calling is to bring glory to the Author of their redemption through lifestyles of worshipful obedience and adoration toward Him. If our behavior is motivated by anything other than the glory of God, then we are not living lives of worship and must be aware that our hearts may have already begun their stumbling digression toward hardness and the eventual leaving of God's values for lesser ones.

We glorify God by living according to the transformation He has wrought for us through the gospel. The New Testament refers to this kind of living as living as saints in a evil world. Now some might be confused by the use of that word *saints*. Some church traditions have relegated that term to deceased people who lived such remarkable lives that a church council somewhere bestowed this status on them, but this is a concept very far removed from the biblical use of the term *saint*. In the New Testament, all who have trusted in Jesus Christ's substitutionary sacrifice for their sins are referred to as saints. In 1 Corinthians 1:2, Paul wrote: "To the church of God which is at Corinth, to those who are sanctified, in Christ Jesus, called to be saints…" In Paul's mind (and he wrote under the inspiration of the Holy Spirit), every person who has entered into a saving relationship with Jesus Christ is a saint. The word in the original Greek for "saint" has the same root word as does the word for holy. That's what saint means, *holy one.* And believers in Jesus Christ are God's holy ones in this world (made holy by Christ's own righteousness imputed to them), in order to bring Him glory and to testify of His grace. Thus, every pursuit of our lives should be subservient to the greater goal of living holy lives for God's glory in this evil world.

In living for God's glory, passionate for holiness, we are called to evangelize the lost. Jesus said to His apostles and all subsequent disciples in Matthew 28:19, "Go, and make disciples of all nations…" Christ, the Head of the Church and the One with all authority, has commanded us to proclaim salvation to those who are ignorant of His salvation. The Bible speaks of the exclusive nature of salvation through Jesus Christ. Any old pathway to God won't do! Christ *alone* is the way to be made right with God, and yet the fallenness of the human heart is perpetually inclined toward making its own way to God through its own efforts and trusting in its own righteousness. Therefore, because of pervasive human spiritual blindness, it is necessary to *tell* people that God has provided a way—a different way, not their way, but *His way*— for those who are outside of a saving relationship with God. They must hear of God's provision in order to flee God's wrath against their sin and trust in Christ's wrath-ending[6] sacrifice at Calvary for their forgiveness and the transformation of their beings. "Faith comes by hearing," Paul reminded us in Romans 10:17.

The nation of Israel had a similar evangelistic calling from God to be a light to the nations. They failed. I often wonder if the church will also fail in her calling. Indeed, in many locations, she is failing. And the reason is our hard-hearted indifference toward the authority of Christ over us and His calling upon us. Oh, we don't see ourselves as hard-hearted. But we choose lesser objectives that take our focus away from obedience to Christ's command. And because it is appropriate to judge the condition of our hearts by the behavior our lives demonstrate (see Proverbs 4:23), honesty compels us to ask an account of ourselves. Are we walking in obedience to Christ's Great Commission? Lack of obedience and a hard-heartedness are often one and the same.

I am not meaning to be rigid or harsh, only truthful. And in the interest of truth and honesty toward God's family, I want you to know that I truly believe that all genuine believers desire to live lives free from spiritual stumbling. But we must also consider that a genuine desire to be free from sin must coexist with an equally strong passion for obedience. You see, it is one thing to dislike the consequences of stumbling, but it is quite another thing to love obedience. We can focus on the cessation of sin until we're blue in the face, but until our unquenchable fleshly appetites are eclipsed by a higher and greater love—the love of the approval of Jesus Christ alone—we will still miss the blessing of God's love relationship with us and His rightful call upon our lives as His children. Loving the Lord our God with all that is within us means ensuring that all other rival loves are put to death.

---

[6] What the New Testament refers to as *propitiation* is defined as a wrath-ending appeasement for sin. See also First John 2:2.

True obedience flows out of a love response to God because of His intervening salvation through Christ. Such a response to God results in a resolve to do what He says no matter the personal costs. Even if it costs friendship, position, influence, or my very life, I will follow Jesus because it is Jesus who gave Himself for me. How can we who have received all Christ has done in our behalf do less than this? Are there any reading this book who would say, *This is the kind of believer I want to be for the glory of my Lord Jesus Christ, who gave Himself fully that I would know God personally and be able to enjoy Him forever?*

So how do we engage such a level of obedience? "Go therefore and make disciples of all the nations" says Matthew 28:19. This is Christ's Great Commission. Sadly, many of God's people read the Great Commission and go on with life, rarely ever thinking of it again. The ignoring of God's commands or the outright rejection of them is something that needs to be recognized, admitted to, and is in need of repentance.

On the other hand, some may have misunderstood the Great Commission, and immediately dismissed it as an outright impossibility. How can any of us go to *all the world*? But this understanding is as wrong as it is simplistic. We cannot dismiss God's commands because our human reasoning has difficulty getting its "arms" around what God has said. Acting that way is, in fact, disobedient living. Rather we must strive to bring our thinking into conformity to God's commands. How is this done?

First, we must interpret Christ's words, not individually, but as the whole Body of Christ. He never spoke to one individual telling him to go to the whole world. Such a premise is physically impossible. Jesus gave His commission to the church, His Body, His redeemed ones of every age and nation and language group. It is our synergistic obedience that He is commanding—*all* of His people in *every* land doing His bidding throughout *every* generation until He comes. If we look at His commission in this light, it is far more likely that we will understand it as being within reason and engage it in obedience. This does not eradicate the necessity for some to dedicate their entire lives to the proclamation of the gospel. Truly God calls some to this distinctive privilege, but the above interpretation of the Great Commission toward the entire Body of Christ (not just a select few) is the normal reading.

This interpretation is underscored further by understanding the impact of the original language for Matthew 28:19. It is the Greek language in which the writers of Scripture wrote, and what they wrote in that language (the Greek, not the English) was inspired by the Holy Spirit in all of its content, down to the word choices and the grammatical form of those words. With that said, we need to understand that what our English Bibles translate as a command is in reality a participle in the Greek. Our Bibles read, "Go and make disciples." *Go* appears to be a command, but that is not the case. The command is *make disciples. Go* is the participle and is more accurately translated, *going* or *as you are going*.

The original language's meaning here is absolutely essential to understand. If people who desire to be obedient to Christ and His commands misunderstand the intent of the original language, we might feel guilty for not being vocational missionaries. But I maintain that God does not want every believer to be a *vocational* missionary. What God wants is for all His people to carry the gospel into the world where He has placed us, having given us skills and abilities to make wealth in this world (one of the messages of Ecclesiastes) and engaging people in our relational contexts with the gospel of Jesus Christ. Thus we are to use all we are—our education, our station in life, our possessions, our friendships, and the power of our influence—to make disciples of people in our everyday life contexts.

If we grasp what our Lord has commanded, that *as we are going* we are to take with us the gospel of Jesus Christ, then it makes all the difference in the world how our lives are managed in light of the hope of eternal life that we bear. As we get up each day to face our normal life contexts, we will carry the message of Christ with us (because it dwells within us) to everyone in our pathway that day.

There is great freedom in being a servant of Jesus Christ, whether or not we derive a paycheck from that service. We are privileged to be Christ's representatives in the world (*our* worlds) where He has placed us to do our daily work, living in daily association with people who need Christ. Knowing that privilege and engaging its calling does not alleviate the reality of the spiritual conflict between the worlds of light and darkness, but the obedient Christian entrusts himself to his Lord who has all power and authority, and will deal with Satan and his influence as He deems appropriate. Our responsibility is to engage His calling with intentionality, with purpose and with passion to those around us.

As a believer and servant of Jesus Christ, there is nothing more worthwhile than to dedicate your whole being to the will of your Master. That is the calling God wants us to comprehend and obey. The lessons learned from Jonah's disobedience ought to help us choose obedience more consistently, laying down our own lives, loving Him more than we love ourselves or any creature comfort this world provides.

One more thing. I promise you that if you evangelize in this world, it is only a matter of time before you also suffer for it. Please don't take my word for it, listen to the words of one of Jesus' closest friends, "For to this you were called, even as Christ also suffered for us, leaving us an example, that you should follow in His steps" (see First Peter 2:21). O precious fellow believer, we are called to glorify God, to live as saints in an evil world, and to engage the Great Commission intentionally, and especially toward those closest to us relationally. In doing so, there will be some amount of suffering involved. It is the nature of living righteously in a fallen, evil world. But choosing the priority of obedience will produce a joy that will more than eclipse the pain of suffering as God's will is engaged.

Do we obediently adhere to the calling of God or are we shunning His calling, running from it like Jonah ran from God's calling upon his life? If the latter describes us, we have already stumbled and there is a growing callousness of heart within us to the ways of God and His priority that people come to know Him. Dear ones, our hearts are stumbling if God has clearly spoken, and we have chosen a different pathway. If we have lost God's heart for His world, we are living inversely to God's priorities as revealed in His Word, living with first things as last and last things as first.

Christians profess to believe that God has spoken in the Bible. We call it His Word. And neither we nor the kingdom of God can afford hard-hearted, willfully stumbling followers of Jesus Christ. People are lost and headed toward eternal punishment and separation from God. Their rescue is in God's hands, to be sure, but He has commissioned *us* with the gospel of salvation. God has spoken. Are we obeying, or have we gone in another direction? Are we living our daily lives as a reflection of God's heart for His world, or are our priorities inverted to reflect lesser motives and objectives?

3
Sleeping While Others Are Perishing

> But Jonah had...lain down, and was fast asleep.
>
> —Jonah 1:5

Recently, while listening to talk radio, I heard of a lifeguard who was fired because he rescued a drowning man. I was incredulous as I listened. It seemed that the problem with the rescue was that the man in need of saving was not in the lifeguard's assigned section. I suppose his authority structure would have preferred him to adopt Jonah's attitude toward dying people. Just turn your head and fall asleep. Professing Christians today have this one down pat! You see, another sign of a heart that is stumbling in its obedience is seen in where Jonah was and what he was doing in the midst of the crisis that threatened the lives of his ship mates. He was asleep. Jonah slept while others were perishing.

Look at what God's word tells us about Jonah as he was with lost people in a situation of peril.

> But the Lord sent out a great wind on the sea, and there was a mighty tempest on the sea, so that the ship was about to be broken up. Then the mariners were afraid;

and every man cried out to his god, and threw the cargo that was in the ship into the sea, to lighten the load. *But Jonah had gone down into the lowest parts of the ship, had lain down, and was fast asleep.* (emphasis mine)
—Jonah 1:4,5

Jonah was so exhausted from all the energy he was expending on running from God that he slept through the storm that threatened to destroy the ship and take the lives of seasoned sailors.

People everywhere, all around us, are lost. We are in the company of people daily who need Christ. The gospel dwells safely inside us as God's people who have received Christ Jesus as our Lord and Savior, but instead of approaching the lost with the concern of God for their souls, our consciousness of their perilous condition has become dulled in our hearts. Instead of telling them of God's plan of rescue, we often sleep the sleep of callousness of heart.

In Jonah's case, he was intentionally avoiding his call from God as he ran in the other direction. Many of us may be doing the same. Have you considered how much energy running from or avoiding God's calling involves? We expend energy on feeding wrong thinking, nurturing anger and bitterness, trying to convince others of our status as victims, and coddling our wounded emotions. All this not only spreads the toxin of a skewed perspective on everyone who comes in contact with us, but exhausts us in a perpetual frenzy of disobedience. Running from God's call expends the energies that would otherwise be used on serving Him, obeying His call. In Jonah's context, the lost were dying (literally), and the prophet of God was asleep. Content to meet his own needs, he rested unconcerned for the eternal plight of those around him.

What Jonah was thinking escapes us. What he *wasn't* thinking is loud and clear. Jonah's sleep indicated that his burden for the lost had long departed. These were sailors who should have heard of Yahweh God from a man like Jonah as their passenger. But what is worse is that his sleep tells us that his conscience no longer felt the emotional tug of its disobedience. He was asleep, both physically and spiritually, and the lost around him were perishing. While the key to their salvation was in Jonah's charge, it was locked up from being proclaimed behind the stumbling hardness of his heart toward God's call.

Are we, as God's people in this day asleep like Jonah? Are we tending to our own needs while the lost around us die in their sins without hearing the way of salvation in Christ? Have we gotten so accustomed to eternally unimportant things being in the place of eternally essential things that we think we are normal in our behavior and pursuits? Are we really so calloused in heart that dying people (people who are outside of Christ's saving grace) should die without hearing from our lips of Christ's saving grace?

As I edit this book one more time, just this week I have heard a news report of a retirement home nurse refusing CPR to a resident who had stopped breathing. The nurse said she was following company protocol (although in reality she was not). The shocking truth is that this nurse sat beside a patient who was in a dire emergency, and without an ounce of human compassion that would have led to offering help, she allowed the person to simply die. Such a scenario is unthinkable, right?

Well, this is exactly what happens when Christians refuse to proclaim the gospel of Christ to the lost around us or when we lose our vision of God's purpose for us on earth. If we can go through our daily routines seeking merely to make a living, and yet be unconcerned for the lost around us, we have fallen asleep. If we can be satisfied to spend our earthly resources on ourselves and not invest in worldwide mission efforts to win the lost, we are asleep. If we can rest comfortably and not weep for those we know who are still outside of Christ, then we are asleep. If we act as if we have forgotten that the lost around us are truly lost, and on their way to spending eternity tormented in flames of punishment, separated from God and from loved ones, without Christ, without hope, and eternally lost, and we *do nothing*, then we are asleep!

But what can we do? First, repent of hard-heartedness and its manifestation of a slothful perspective toward God's agenda. Peter proclaimed in Acts 3:19, "Repent...that times of refreshing may come to you from the presence of the Lord." *Times of refreshing* is synonymous with the fruit of obedience. Once your heart turns in the direction of obeying the Lord instead of forsaking His commands, you are ready for some very practical suggestions.

Learn to share your faith. If you have truly been redeemed through a saving relationship with Jesus Christ, you have also inherited the privilege, as well as the responsibility of obeying Christ's commands to evangelize the lost. Think about your own salvation experience. Aren't you glad someone obeyed the Lord when they told *you* about Him? You should count it a privilege to go and do the same. Jesus said, "Freely you have received, freely give" (Matthew 10:8).

Prepare and practice giving your personal testimony. Your testimony will be the door that will open further opportunities to share the gospel of Christ with others. People can argue your theology all day long, but no one can put forth a valid argument to disassemble what has happened in your life personally. During my military career, I worked in a fighter squadron in the area of aircraft maintenance. There was a limited amount of down time for flight line personnel just before the aircraft were scheduled to land. When all the preparations for aircraft recovery were complete, we frequently found ourselves in conversation about different subjects and I often asked the Lord to turn the topic toward eternal matters. He faithfully did this, and one day as we were awaiting our returning aircraft one such discussion evolved. I sought to give a clear explanation of the gospel of Christ, but every point I made was immediately (and with a visible measure of animosity) countered by one young soldier. Finally, my inner frustration spilled over and I said with much conviction, "Well, Christ truly changed *my* life, and you can't dispute *that*." His response shocked me. "Well, you got me there," he said. That day I learned a new lesson about how powerful a personal testimony can be.

Another way of meeting and sharing Christ with the lost is to open your home in hospitality. Invite people over for dinner, coffee or tea and snacks. Food seems to disarm apprehension. Everyone loves to eat. Often sitting around food or at a meal together provides a more natural avenue for conversation in an environment of acceptance and warmth. All of us have friends, work acquaintances, and neighbors that need to know Christ. Have them into your homes and show them genuine Christian love through hospitality.

Force yourselves to step out of your comfort zone. I say "force" because that's usually what needs to happen. Because we are comfortable with our comfort zones (redundancy intended), it doesn't happen naturally that we step outside of them. If you always remain where you're comfortable, you will rarely reach the lost or even minimally affect them. Can you hand a tract to a teller, a toll taker, a grocery store clerk? Can you see someone having a bad day and offer to pray for them? Do you pray before a meal in a restaurant? Can you offer to pray for the server concerning his or her needs? You might be surprised at the spiritual readiness of some people if God's people would just think of others a little more than themselves, step outside of their comfort zones, and express genuine Christlike concern. Perhaps the reason we don't see God doing more to bring people to Christ is because we are not doing what He has called us to do in expressing genuine love and concern toward them in life's normal contexts.

Can you sit with an elderly person, listening to them reminisce? Can you hold the hand of a suffering person who is in need of emotional support? Can you extend the love of Christ to hurting or grieving people with a warm handshake, an inviting smile, or an embrace of empathy? It might surprise some of us at how responsive people might be if they observed a genuine demonstration of the love of Christ being shared in practical ways from those who claim to be His people.

Without meaning to sound legalistic or putting you on a false guilt trip (I don't mind the true guilt that comes from the Holy Spirit), the reality is that most of us can do much more than we do. God's calling for us and His agenda for the world is that the lost hear of Christ, that *His salvation* should take center stage on the earth and in our lives.

In the spirit of John the Baptist who said that we should bring forth fruit in keeping with our repentance, make a commitment to God as a result of lessons learned from His Word. Admit to God that you need Him to realign your heart with His heart for the lost. Then do something practical and perhaps even a bit radical. Make a list of people you know of who need to know Jesus Christ as their Lord and Savior. Start with just five, but don't limit it to that number. Then ask God regularly for their salvation and invite Him to use you to tell them about Christ.

Do you think God wants to answer that prayer? Of course He does. You can expect Him to. The Scriptures assure us of God's heart for the lost. Second Peter 3:9 reminds us that "[the Lord] is long-suffering toward us, not willing that *any* should perish, but that *all* should come to repentance." The Apostle John (First John 2:2) also weighs in with these words, "And He Himself is the propitiation for our sins, and not for ours only but also *for the whole world.*" (emphases in both verses mine). O, People of God, let us not sleep while others are perishing.

4
Giving Lip-Service to Following God in the Midst of Rebellion

> Then they said to him, "Please tell us!
> For whose cause is this trouble upon us?
> What is your occupation? And where do you come from?
> What is your country? And of what people are you?"
> So he said to them, "I am a Hebrew; and I fear the Lord,
> the God of heaven, who made the sea and the dry land."
>
> —Jonah 1:8-12

During my military days, Christian fellowship was rare, yet sought for. I looked carefully for others who also confessed Christ as Savior. One such guy was as vocal about his relationship with God as I was, yet in time I discovered that his behavior did not reinforce his claims. One day we were being transported by military vehicle from one area of the flight line to another. Because of the short ride most of us were simply piled into the back of the truck, but my "Christian" friend took a seat in the cab with the driver. He didn't realize that a window in the rear of the cab made his actions visible to everyone in the back. As we rode from point A to point B, he unashamedly perused pornographic magazines, occasionally holding up a picture for the driver and (unknown to him) those in the back to see. The comments from the unsaved men in the back gave astounding evidence to the unfolding destruction of this man's testimony by his hypocritical actions. Jonah demonstrated this same indication of a hardened, stumbling heart when he gave lip-service to knowing God in the midst of his rebellious flight from God.

After struggling with keeping the ship afloat in the terrible storm, the crew in desperation came to Jonah, awakened him, and, no doubt, speaking in volumes rivaling the wind and crashing waves, said, "Please tell us! For whose cause is this trouble upon us? What is your occupation? And where do you come from? What is your country? And of what people are you?" And Jonah responded with a very pious, "I am a Hebrew, and I fear the Lord, the God of heaven, who made the sea and the dry land." You've got to be kidding! Who does Jonah think he's fooling? He's on this ship precisely because He was *running* from God, not *serving* Him. And he has the audacity to give lip-service regarding his allegiance to God?

Lest any reader wonder of what I speak, *lip-service* is condemned by Jesus with these words, "These people draw near to Me with their mouths, and honor Me with their lips, but their heart is far from Me" (Matthew 15:8). Defined by Jesus then, lip-service is a disconnect between the profession of the lips and the reality of the heart—what we *say* and what we *do*. Lip-service to serving God is a mere declaration of allegiance to God without the substantive behavioral reality to back it up. Jonah claimed to fear God, but his actions demonstrated that in reality he feared God very little. Self-absorbed and self-deceived, and in the midst of running from God's call, he had the audacity to say that he served the God of the storm.

Keeping up appearances while our hearts are not consecrated to God is hypocrisy. The all-seeing eyes of God, before whom each of us will someday stand, will bring such behavior into account. How is it with you? How is the relationship between your lips and your heart? Your talk and your walk? Ezekiel 36:23 was given to God's people who were suffering captivity in Babylon because of their repeated rebellion against Him and their seared consciences toward holiness.

> And I will sanctify My great name, which has been profaned among the nations, which *you have profaned* in their midst; and the nations shall know that I am the Lord," says the Lord, "When I am hallowed *in you* before their eyes." (emphasis added)

The calling of God for the lives of His people – those making a claim to being followers of Christ – is to hallow God. And the implication from the context is that He is hallowed through our consecrated behavior, behavior that reflects the majestic and magnanimous Person of God who resides within us and sits on the throne of our hearts. Anything less is hypocrisy or mere lip-service to God. We further stumble when we give lip-service to following God while the true condition of our hearts is callousness toward God, His call, and the people to whom we are called to share the gospel.

5
Choosing Death Over Repentance

"Pick me up and throw me into the sea"

—Jonah 1:12

As the story concerning Jonah continues to unfold, it is worth noting that once it was exposed that Jonah himself was the reason for the storm, he did not ask for the crew to try turning the ship around so they could return to port and get Jonah heading in the proper direction. Turning himself around was not part of his thinking. Repentance was not even the smallest blip on his radar.

Jonah chose instead to go overboard to end his life. Remember his level of awareness. He didn't know the big fish was coming to preserve his life. His assumption was that in being thrown overboard, he would drown. And this is the fourth indication of the heart-numbing presence of a stumbling obedience: when we would rather die than repent.

How could dying seem better than turning from one's sins? The digression of a hard, stumbling heart is manifested in full when our own will and perspective is worth dying for, even when there is a more obvious and sensible solution. It is what we insist upon to the "nth degree," the hill that we die on.

Repentance requires a brokenness of spirit that ceases to be concerned with the way self will be perceived. Genuine, biblical repentance will stand in the light of God's conviction and will admit sin, disregarding the perceived potential shunning or condemnation we think will happen as sin comes to light. There is the reality that people will now see us as we truly are, and this reality is often much too much for some in this hardened state to endure. Therefore, they refuse repentance, choosing instead a course that will lead to further death of their spirits before God.

In my years as a pastor, I never ceased to be amazed at the people I met, people *in* the church, who claimed to know and love the Lord Jesus, and yet when confronted about a sin or some spiritually aberrant behavior, would do anything but repent. In fact, most times an insistence on their own way was preferred, even after it became apparent to them (and everyone around them) that they were wrong. The choice not to repent but to foster hardness of heart is the pinnacle of stumbling and is a very dangerous and destructive state of heart. Such a situation should never be tolerated in one's self, nor should it lack a loving confrontation when it is observed in others.

Beloved, are you so distraught that death seems like the only way out? Has your life taken on such a dysfunction that you see no way out but the ultimate relief? Perhaps you are already experiencing the death of your heart's responsiveness to God. It manifests itself in the attitude of *I just cannot change at this point*. If you honestly examine your heart in light of the teaching of chapter one of Jonah, it may be that you will see the same pathway in yourself that you see in Jonah – a departure from God's clear revelation. Somewhere there is an area of disobedience to something God has clearly said; where a pathway other than God's was chosen.

That wrong choice or series of wrong choices led to insensitivity to the true calling of God for your life, which resulted in an unhealthy focus on yourself.

In John 15, Jesus spoke of abiding in Him. He used the term ten times in such phrases as "Abide in Me and I in you;" "Abide in Me and My word in you;" and "Abide in My love." Then He summed them up with, "That your joy may be full." For some believers, the joy of Christ may have long since departed, eclipsed by inverted values and disobedient choices. What should have been an obedient response to God's call was in reality a turning from obedience into a path of human wisdom or some path that seemed right, but its way was the way of death. At the very least, such a death will be the death of one's ability to hear God's voice and respond in obedience. It could be a physical death if self-destruction goes far enough.

The need is for repentance. But if stumbling has displayed its full anatomy in your life, repentance will probably be resisted. This is why I have sought to convince you of the reality of a hard, stumbling heart by the indications given us in chapter one of Jonah's testimony. I know God's Word is powerful and will bring conviction. The question is, are we listening to His voice?

I want you to feel more than conviction, though, I want you to know *hope*. Remember Peter's admonition in Acts 3:19, that repentance brings *times of refreshment from God*? Isn't that what you need most? Don't you want refreshment from God's unhindered presence in your life? It is God's divine work in your heart that alone will be the true remedy for your heart's spiritual dysfunction.

I don't believe a true believer ever intends for his heart to grow cold and hard. But it can happen. The issue of hardness of heart is not to be taken lightly. It may be that you can look back on your life and see that there has *never* been a time of responsiveness to God. If this is the case, you should stop everything you are doing and fall on your knees before almighty God in repentance and cry out for His mercy because you are still under His holy condemnation for your sins. Avoiding divine condemnation requires entering into a genuine, saving relationship with God through His Son, Jesus Christ.

What if you've been in the church all your life but have realized that you're in need of genuinely being saved? I hope you wait no longer, but humble yourself, put off the shell of religion, and come to Jesus Christ in a fresh and vital relationship of surrender to His Lordship. Ask Him to be your Savior by running up the white flag of your heart to His sovereign Lordship. In reality, there cannot be one without the other, for if He truly is your hope for eternal salvation, you will release all of life to His control.

Proverbs 28:13 says, "He who covers his sin will not prosper; but he who confesses and forsakes them will have mercy." Confess your sins, agreeing with God about what has offended Him. Forsake your sins, clinging only to Him. And let Him fill you with Himself. He and He alone is the fountain of living water.

PART 3

*God's Discipline
and the Servant's
Restoration*

Jonah 1:17 - 4:11

6
Swallowed Up in God's Discipline

Jonah 1:17 – 2:9

My childhood had many instances that were less than shining moments. I mean, as much as I hated getting disciplined, my childishly self-centered heart led me to actions that sometimes stirred up my parents' anger. But it wasn't until *after* my parents' wrath was kindled that my heart awakened to their perspective in my wrong. My parents were far from perfect, but the memories of growing up in their home are anchored in the reality of a consistency regarding disobedience, that when it was discovered, it would be punished. Why? Because I was *their* son, and they took their responsibility seriously to raise me to know right and wrong.

In much the same way, the Bible affirms that it is the genuine children of God who experience God's loving, fatherly hand of discipline. Consider Hebrews 12:5,6, "My son, do not despise the discipline of the Lord, nor be discouraged when you are rebuked by Him; for whom the Lord loves He disciplines, and scourges every son whom He receives."

Discipline is exactly the kind of thing that loving parents do to their children when they step out of line. It is a mark of connection between the lover and the ones loved. Hebrews continues (12:7), "If you endure discipline, God deals with you as with sons; for what son is there whom a father does not discipline?"

Mothers sometimes say things to their children out of exasperation that sound like this: *Just wait until your father gets home.* I don't know about the majority of you reading this book, but when my mother said that, it struck fear in my heart and made me wonder why I had pushed her so far. My dad was stronger. His longer arm and bigger muscles meant that his disciplinary "swing" had more impact, and his sessions of discipline usually lasted longer. He desired not just to punish me, but to also instruct me in right and wrong and the need to make good choices. He tried to make his disciplinary words sink down into my soul so that I would one day live on my own, self-governed by what was right and good. And above all, I hated to disappoint my dad. There was something that deeply disturbed my heart, even as a child, at the realization that I had caused my father grief in having to discipline me.

We saw in previous chapters how Jonah rebelled against the Lord to the point of needing the discipline of God. When we speak of discipline, the Scriptures instruct us concerning two kinds: *instructive* and *corrective* discipline. Instructive discipline is the response to the Word of God by engaging our cognitive skills. We learn through God's Word's instruction, then make right choices, accompanied with humble yet distinctive behavioral changes. *Corrective discipline,* on the other hand, involves a response to that which God sovereignly brings into our lives to correct our wandering hearts. Because we are learning from Jonah's experience with God, I am focusing on this second aspect of discipline which comes upon us because we have willingly stepped outside the boundaries of God's will.

We are always free to choose the pathway of disobedience or rebellion. But we are not free to choose the consequences. They are divinely set. So in making our self-centered choices, we can be assured that Father is "coming home" to take care of His erring child. Jonah had run from God in the rebellion of his hard heart. He had received a clear word from God, but had chosen a different pathway. He had expended so much energy on running from God that he was able to sleep while others were perishing. When he was asked about the identity of his god, he responded with a disingenuous and hypocritical lip-service regarding being a servant of God, even while in the midst of actions that demonstrated rebellion against Him. And in what he thought would be the end, he chose to die rather than to repent.

Jonah's heart was stumbling and yet the degree of its hardness escaped him. That's usually the way it is. That's why an area of hardness in our hearts requires divine intervention and that is what we see in Jonah's account. We pick up the narrative at the point where he is cast into the sea and God provides a creative alternative to death, a giant sea creature to swallow Jonah and be a divinely orchestrated "time out," a significant three-day time of reflection.

Jonah's disciplinary experience is well worth a serious examination, for in so doing we will learn much about God's discipline in our own lives, a discipline that every true child of God will experience at one time or another.

God is the Author of Discipline

> Now *the Lord had prepared a fish* to swallow Jonah. And Jonah was in the belly of the fish three days and three nights. (emphasis added)
> —Jonah 1:17

To even the most casual reader, it is obvious that this was not a happenstance of misfortune that befell Jonah. It was the plan of God for an errant prophet. God's discipline is part of His plan for all His children.

I dare say that there are many times that we misunderstand the discipline of the Lord. We may call the adversity of divine discipline *bad luck*, or we may wrongly think we have fallen out of favor with the Lord. But neither of these perspectives is correct. If God is sovereign, how can there be any such thing as *luck* in the life of someone guided by this sovereign Lord of the universe? And if we are His children by the covenant made through His only begotten Son, our Lord Jesus Christ, how can we fall out of favor with God?

We must first look at the covenant under which Jonah ministered, God's favor was on Israel because of Himself. Consider Deuteronomy 7:7-8:

> The Lord did not set His love on you nor choose you because you were more in number than any other people, for you were the least of all peoples; but because the Lord loved you, and because He would keep the oath which He swore to your fathers, the Lord has brought you out with a mighty hand, and redeemed you from the hand of Pharaoh king of Egypt.

The favor of God on Israel was due simply because of the purposes of God in covenant, and not their performance or obedience. In fact, they seldom kept their end of the covenant. But God is faithful to Himself and to His own name by keeping covenant with His people.

> Can a woman forget her nursing child,
> And not have compassion on the son of her womb?
> Surely they may forget, yet I will not forget you.
> See, I have inscribed you on the palms of My hands.[7]

Precious people of God, it is precisely *because* we are in God's favor that He disciplines His own beloved children. This is such an important truth for God's people to grasp that Hebrews 12:8 takes this truth and enshrouds it in family-type language that we can all understand. "But if you are without discipline, of which all have become partakers, then you are illegitimate children and not sons."

As believers, we are God's beloved children. No longer are we distant from God, standing afar off and approaching God through the mediation of a human priest. In the New Covenant through Christ Jesus, we who were aliens, orphaned, and cast away from God are now beloved children of God. We who were afar off have been brought near. And because of these things, we may address the God of the universe as *Father.* We are His children by right of adoption and by purchase of redemption. *Father* is a term of endearment, indicative of the relationship of intimacy we now enjoy as His children through Christ Jesus. And God our Father is the author of discipline in our lives precisely because we who are born from above are in covenant relationship with Him as His beloved children.

Think about it like this: you do not discipline *all* the children of the neighborhood, but only those children with whom you have an intimate, blood covenant relationship. That is precisely the way it is with God as *our* Father. And in this Father/child relationship

---

[7] Isaiah 49:15

between God and His redeemed children, He fulfills His right and responsibility to bring us up to know and walk in His ways. And that means that at times, we will require the strong arm of His fatherly discipline because of our errant ways. In short, discipline for the child of God is from the hand of God – a kind, fatherly, benevolent, and merciful hand – because of our covenant relationship with Him.

God's Discipline is Purposeful

Divine discipline is an assurance of God's covenant relationship with us. Hebrews 12:6 reminds us, "For whom the Lord loves, He disciplines." The discipline of our own children followed what we understood of God's dealings with us, that His corrective measures were purposeful: to restore the intimacy of the relationship and to invoke a higher level of responsibility. And discipline in that vein is always accompanied by assurances of love.

The prayer Jonah prayed in the midst of his discipline reveals significant heart issues that Jonah needed to come to grips with. God was intent on bringing him to the point of dealing with these heart issues. Perhaps some of us need those same lessons. Let us give heed to the lessons Jonah learned in the purposeful discipline in which he found himself.

God is Near to His Children

Jonah learned that even in the adversity of divine discipline that God's ear is turned toward His children. "I cried out to the Lord because of my affliction, and *He answered me*. Out of the belly of Sheol I cried, and *You heard my voice*" (Jonah 2:2, emphasis mine).

It must be logically determined that Jonah wrote this from a point subsequent to his discipline, as it would have been impossible for him to set up table and chair, light a candle, and take pen in hand while in the belly of the sea creature. But even in this reflective mode sometime after the fact, as he remembered God's dealings with him he could see God's compassionate heart toward him to hear his cry for help, even in a disciplinary situation that came upon him because of his own rebellion. If we understand that divine discipline is, indeed, a merciful expression of God's heart toward His own, that understanding ought to lead us to join the psalmist's adoration as he said in Psalm 116:1,2, "I love the Lord because He has heard my voice and my supplication; because He has inclined His ear to me, therefore I will call upon Him as long as I live." God is near to His people, even in a disciplinary situation.

In the intensity of God's discipline, our emotions can convince us that the end is near, while God's Word tells us that the discipline is merely a step in the growth process through which God the Father is taking us. In discipline our emotions dictate that we are the objects of God's wrath, but the reality is that we are objects of love and the discipline is the primary evidence of that love.

God's heart in discipline is to restore the intimacy of the Father/child relationship. That means that the Father's ear is perpetually turned toward His beloved covenant people. I remember instances when our own kids had been disciplined. It was important to us as the ones who had administered the discipline to keep our ears tuned in the direction of our children, amid and after the discipline. Their *cries* invoked our compassion, but their *words* revealed to our spirits whether or not their hearts were turning back toward conformity to our family's (and God's) expectations. This is the first lesson to which Jonah makes reference in his prayer. In the midst of the consequences of his rebellion, access to God's ear did not have to be earned or cajoled. God's ear, like a concerned and responsible parent, was already inclined toward His erring child.

God Rules the Lives of His Servants

Jonah's second lesson concerning God's discipline took shape as he reflected on his near death experience, being reminded of God's sovereign rule over his life. He says, "For You cast me into the deep, into the heart of the seas, and the floods surrounded me; all Your billows and Your waves passed over me" (Jonah 2:3).

Notice how Jonah attributes the details of his debacle to God's sovereign activity. Even though the crew of the ship actually threw him in, he says, "*You* cast me into the deep." On the day of the disaster, he simply saw a raging ocean, but upon reflection, he understood, "*Your* billows and *Your* waves passed over me." Even though he was trying to escape from the presence of the Lord (Jonah 1:3), in the fish's belly he discovered afresh what David had written in Psalm 139:7 some 200 years earlier, "Where can I go from Your Spirit? Or where can I flee from Your presence?"

Wherever we run, we find that God is there because He does not break covenant with us. And while humans are perpetual covenant breakers, God is a perpetual covenant keeper because of His nature to be faithful. Second Timothy 2:13 unequivocally affirms that "if we are faithless, He remains faithful; for He cannot deny Himself." Because of his experience under divine discipline, Jonah understood on a new level God's sovereign and faithful rule over the details of his life.

In the belly of the fish our erring prophet understood afresh that his life was in God's hands. While Jonah tried to be his own master, he was divinely reminded (and rather sternly at that) that God is the true Lord and Ruler of his life. Take note of the hopeless feelings he recalls as he remembers his plunge into the depths of the sea.

> Then I said, 'I have been cast out of Your sight; yet I will look again toward Your holy temple.' The waters

> surrounded me, even to my soul; the deep closed around me; weeds were wrapped around my head. I went down to the moorings of the mountains; the earth with its bars closed behind me forever.
> —Jonah 2:4-6

These words clearly communicate that Jonah thought he was in his last seconds of life. Then the creature came along and swallowed him.

Try to put yourself in Jonah's place for a moment. Wasn't it bad enough to be dying from drowning? But that didn't happen instantly. Holding his breath as long as he could, he sank down into the depths, all the way to the bottom where the growth of weeds entangled themselves around him. He was driven and tossed and held down by the current which was too strong to overcome. Then, just when he was out of breath and thought that death from drowning was about to overtake him, he was gulped down by a sea creature.

Can you imagine how utterly terrified he must have been? And equally as shocking must have been the realization (only a few seconds later) that he was still alive, and that there was air enough to breathe inside this creature's stomach, albeit not very pleasant air, to be sure. And as he later reflected on those thoughts of twice being near death, at the crescendo of all he felt he says in verse 6 of chapter 2, "Yet You have brought up my life from the pit, O Lord, my God." Jonah understood afresh that even in discipline, his life was in God's hands.

A New Level of Dependency

Jonah also learned to embrace the posture of dependency upon God, the God of all creation, who also held every detail of *his life* in His sovereign and all-powerful hands. In his situation of discipline he realized just how much he needed God, that being in the midst of God's discipline meant an unpleasant and unwelcome distance between him and God. As he realized (finally!) what a dire thing it is to be apart from the presence of the Lord, Jonah exclaimed with renewed passion for the presence of God in his life, "O Lord, my God" (cf. Jonah 2:6). Notice the difference between this statement and the way he refers to God in 1:9 of his writing. Before his discipline he referred to God with the phrase, *the God of heaven*. This is a true enough description of God, but it is also a rather innocuous and distant title, one reflecting Jonah's heart's distance from God at the time. But by the way God is now being addressed in 2:6, the dependency of his soul upon God has been rekindled. What was a mere glowing ember is now a flaming fire, and all because of God's discipline upon his life. God is not just God over all of creation, but He is "the Lord, *my* God." Notice more of his statements of dependency in his prayer:

> I cried out to the Lord because of my affliction (2);
> Yet I will look again toward Your holy temple (4);
> You have brought up my life from the pit (6);
> and I remembered the Lord; my prayer went up to You,
> into Your holy temple (7).

One of the primary purposes of God's discipline is to restore us to our rightful position of dependency. Straying from that dependency deceptively feels like freedom, but it always ends in death – the death of intimacy with God (at the very least) or in the worst case scenario, the death of the person himself. Because God is unchanging in His goodness and unfailing in His love, He is committed to bringing His erring children back to a relationship of dependency.

As Americans, we highly value independence. But as Christians, we should value *dependency*. To be independent of God is to be foolish, rebellious, and even idolatrous. But when we are disciplined by God, He restores us to a position of dependency. And growing in utter dependency upon God is not only a great lesson, a lesson filled with immeasurable joy, but is the only position whereby we can be free to be all that God has created us to be and to rightly enjoy our relationship with our Creator.

Jonah's embracing of the lesson of dependency meant that he personally understood what God had said to Abraham centuries earlier, "*I* am your...exceedingly great reward" (Genesis 15:1). God's purposeful discipline brings forth the fruit of understanding that God Himself is the greatest, most blessed reward to our souls. He alone is incomparable in value to anything we could imagine. Knowing *Him*, loving *Him*, and serving *Him* is in fact the fulfillment of that for which we were created. And there is no deeper, more abiding joy than this realization.

As Jonah was disciplined by God, he learned that God's ear is turned toward His children, even in rebellion; that God is sovereign over life; that He holds life in His hands; and that he was to rely upon God in complete and utter dependency.

New Priorities

Jonah then responded with a very natural next step – he ordered his life according to the purposes of God. Corrective discipline comes upon the child of God precisely because he has stepped outside of God's will. And when we respond properly to God's discipline, our lives take on a new order, a revised priority that reflects God's purposes being lived out in our lives. This is taught in the New Testament as well: "All discipline for the moment seems not to be joyful, but sorrowful; yet to those who have been trained by it, it yields the peaceful fruit of righteousness" (cf. Hebrews 12:11).

To order one's life also includes a return to a posture of grateful worship. In verse 8 of his prayer, Jonah states, "Those who regard worthless idols forsake their own Mercy." Whatever went on in his heart that was at the root of his rebellion, Jonah calls it as it is, "worthless idols." And he continues in verse 9: "But I will sacrifice to You with the voice of thanksgiving." His heart is now ordered according to the purpose for which he was created, to come before his Maker in dependency offering himself for God's purposes in a posture of grateful worship.

To order one's life also means a decision to do the right thing. Notice the *I wills* of chapter 2 after Jonah has come to terms with his sin. "I will pay what I have vowed," can be interpreted this way: *There was a day when God called and I said "Yes." But I have foolishly turned away from that calling. I will now, as a result of God's gracious dealing with me, return to obeying what I know God has called me to do.*

When God's discipline has had its purifying work in our hearts, an orderly life of obedience is the result. It is an obedience that is more intentional and more pure than it was before. In the wake of his discipline from God, Jonah made a conscious decision to do the right thing, the thing God had called him to do in the first place. He said, "I will pay what I have vowed."

Taking It To Heart

Sometimes even genuine Christians, God's true children, can wander in the emotional turmoil of God's discipline. Confusion and feelings of hopelessness may try to assail the heart and unravel the thinking, even to the point of causing one to give up trying any longer to be a Christian. The answer does not lie in continuing to listen to your renegade emotions. An objective decision needs to be made—the same decision Jonah made. Raise the white flag of surrender in your heart and return to a life of dependency upon God.

Don't wait until you can figure out the whole path to recovery. Make a decision today to walk in the truths that God has shown you through His holy Word. Obey God in what you know and you will be amazed at how those old emotions will somehow be eclipsed by a victory in your life – a victory that only repentance and faith in God can bring.

Such a firm decision is reflected in the lyrics of this hymn:

> I am resolved no longer to linger,
> charmed by the world's delight;
> things that are higher, things that are nobler,
> these have allured my sight.
>
> I am resolved to follow the Savior,
> faithful and true each day;
> heed what He saith, do what He willeth,
> He is the living way.[8]

Jonah's return to intimacy with God was through the lessons he learned in his disciplinary experience. And we who are God's beloved children would find ourselves prudent if we heeded these lessons as well.

Discipline is Also Mercy

There is one more observation about God's discipline that I want you to see. I hope you plant this truth deeply into your heart. It is this: God's discipline is measured out to His child according to the need of the erring heart. This is an amount that only God can know. Observe 2:10, "So the Lord spoke to the fish, and it vomited Jonah onto dry land." At such a time as only His all-seeing, all-

---

[8] Hymn, "I Am Resolved" by Palmer Hartsough. Public Domain.

knowing eyes could see, God determined that Jonah had learned his lessons. Jonah had repented, therefore the discipline was over and God commanded the creature to give him up.

This is indeed another demonstration of the mercy and sovereignty of God! The fish didn't just lose its lunch in the ocean, leaving Jonah to his own devices for getting to land. God didn't cause the fish to throw Jonah up and then say to Jonah: *Well, I saved your life, now swim, fool!* No. God tenderly and meticulously orchestrated every detail of his ordeal for Jonah's good. He directed the creature to beach itself, and at the proper time, when Jonah could be safe from drowning, God caused the creature to give a great heave. God saw to it that His child, who was the object of His loving and Fatherly discipline, was mercifully deposited on the land.

We can say, then, with confidence that God's discipline is another facet of His mercy. God mercifully ensured that Jonah was redeposited onto the land. The land is the place where he departed from God's calling. The land is the place where he could get a fresh start. It was on the land that his calling could resume and where obedience could take its rightful place under the will and direction of God. And the land was the place where Jonah could reorder his life according to eternity's values. And when *we* experience God's discipline that is what God does for us as well. When His discipline has run its course, and when we have learned the lessons He intends, He will see to it that we are redeposited at a place where we can resume following Him.

How is it with you today? Is your life hard? Is it *divinely* hard? Do you believe you may be under God's discipline for turning from His clear Word? Remember the lessons of this prophet's life, that discipline is from God's benevolent hand toward His covenant children, that God's discipline is purposeful for our growth, and that it is measured out according to the need of your heart.

Your response should be as distinct and intentional as it is simple, *surrender*. Surrender your all to your Master for His use, so that the remainder of your days are spent with eternity's values in view. And eternity's values are that for which you were created, that which is for your best, and the values for which your redeemed heart truly longs. You will never be satisfied with anything other than God. And His discipline is His purposeful intervention to restore your intimacy with Him. It is as Augustine once wrote in prayer to God: "Our hearts are restless until they find their rest in Thee."[9]

Surrender was never more beautifully described as in the old hymn that has been a part of so many of our lives.

> Have Thine own way, Lord, have Thine own way.
> Thou art the Potter; I am the clay.
> Mold me and make me after Thy will
> While I am waiting yielded and still.
>
> Have Thine own way, Lord, have Thine own way.
> Hold o'er my being absolute sway.
> Fill with Thy Spirit till all shall see
> Christ only, always, living in me.[10]

---

[9] St. Augustine. *The Confessions of St. Augustine Bishop of Hippo, Vol. I,* Chapter 1.

[10] Hymn, "Have Thine Own Way, Lord." Adelaide A. Pollard; George C. Stebbins. Public Domain.

7

The God of the Second Chance

and the third, and the fourth, and the fifth...
Jonah 2:10 – 3:10

Nothing is more welcome news than the announcement that the exam we forgot to study for will be given again, and only the highest grade from the two tests will be made permanent. When we speak unkindly and it is forgiven and the relationship is restored, we are grateful for the practical expression of committed love and its invitation to try again to live in harmony with the one who was offended. God's second chances; we need them.

Let me tell you about one of my own second chances. Rod was new to our fighter squadron. I was assigned to accompany him in order to orient him to our base, the necessary offices and their locations so that he might complete his in-processing. Rod and I were together often and we became comfortable with one another. It was apparent he was not a Christian and the Spirit of God impressed me many times to initiate a conversation with him about his need for a saving relationship with God. My thinking was that we had time. I would share Christ with him eventually, but it was important to build bridges of friendship. I waited but my waiting was more out of resistance and disobedience than it was a genuine search for opportunities to tell him about Christ. In fact, opportunities were there repeatedly, but I chose not to take them. One morning at role call (the beginning of our military work day), with great sadness in his voice, our flight sergeant announced Rod's sudden death the night before from a heart attack. He was 23.

My personal grief overwhelmed my heart from two directions, for not only had I lost a new friend, but I had an incredible guilt in my spirit from resistance to God's voice regarding Rod's need for salvation. There is much to relate regarding the lessons God pressed to my heart through this experience, but the main one to share with you here is that in those days I resolved to change my behavior in anticipation of God's second chance. When in future circumstances I perceived God opening a relational door for the gospel, I determined that never again would I miss an opportunity to share Christ's grace with a lost person.

Second chances are always welcome simply because we are so adept at blowing our first chances. Failure of any kind is fertile ground for the forgiveness and restoration inherent in the second chance. Second chances are expressions of the mercy of our God. Mercy was surely extended to me in my disobedience, although disciplinary judgment was deserved. Yet God's mercy, shown toward this sluggish and resistant servant, taught me much that has translated into a greater resolve toward obedience. His mercy is so very difficult to comprehend, yet so consistently revealed in Scripture as available and sufficient for us.

Why does God love humanity so? Why would He who has been so profoundly offended by our sinful condition, as well as our perpetually sinful ways, want to extend mercy and forgiveness to us? These questions are an astonishing mystery and are not easily answered. Yet what is revealed in Scripture is enough to make us ready, willing, and even anxious to receive it. To the sinner who has come to realize his true condition before God's all-seeing eyes, the mercy of God is an oasis of hope in a barren desert of despair, self-condemnation, and hopelessness.

As we study Jonah's experience, the window into God's heart is opened a bit further, expanding our understanding of His incredible mercy towards His people. Such understanding empowers us to reach out and embrace His love and heart in our own need for mercy.

Look at the opening verse to chapter three: "Now the word of the Lord came to Jonah *a second time*" (emphasis added). Did you catch that? God hands Jonah the equivalent of an engraved invitation to obey His original instruction. It wasn't something God had to do, and it certainly wasn't deserved on Jonah's part. God could have annihilated him and would have been perfectly just in doing so, but instead He issued another opportunity to obey. That's the way God is. His heart is inclined to be merciful toward His servants, even when they disobey Him.

"Failures" That God Still Used

Scripture is replete with examples of men who failed, and yet God extended to them His gracious, fatherly hand – reproving their sin, correcting their errors, lifting them up, giving them renewed stability, and reestablishing their walks into a more faithful pattern.

Consider some examples from biblical history of God's second chances. Abraham lied about Sarah being his wife and almost caused her to be defiled in a pagan king's harem. In the Ishmael incident, he tried to fulfill God's promise through human means (that never works, by the way). Yet, because of God's merciful actions toward him, he became the father of those who come to God in faith through Christ Jesus (see Galatians 3:7).

Abraham's second chance from God was not an isolated case. It seems to be a pattern with God. Remember Jacob, the schemer who deceived his father and swindled his brother? God gave him another opportunity and he eventually became the patriarch of the nation of Israel.

How about Samson? He was a man who consistently failed God because he couldn't manage his hormones. Yet in God's second chances, he is used to deliver Israel from the oppressing hand of the Philistines.

David, though remembered in Scripture as the sweet psalmist of Israel and the man after God's own heart, was also an adulterer and a murderer. Yet he was God's man through covenant, and divine mercy was extended to him repeatedly.

Then there was Peter. Many of us identify readily with him. Peter was a curious blend of courage and insecurity, dependability and wishy-washiness. On the night of the Lord's betrayal and arrest, when Jesus could have used the support and allegiance of His disciples, Peter was overcome with the fear of being discovered as a disciple, then arrested and possibly executed. Thus in one of the most notable occasions of self-preservation in biblical history, Peter denied His Lord. Yet Jesus, the express image of our merciful God, restored him so much so that he became a pillar of leadership for the early church.

The apostle Paul, "blessed" with a driven, type A personality, is found to be at odds with the gentle and compassionate Barnabas. The account in Acts 15 reveals that this was a profound problem between the two of them. In fact, the personal conflict between them became so emotionally inflamed that Paul deemed Barnabas unfit as a missionary team member unless he acquiesced to his perspective. And in one of the first recorded accounts of trouble between two motivated Christian missionaries, their personal disagreement became such an insurmountable obstacle that they saw no other alternative but to part ways from one another. Yet God extended to Paul His mercy. And who would deny his usefulness? He became a phenomenal church planter, authoring thirteen books of the New Testament (three epistles we no longer have[11]) and God only knows what else.

Furthermore, let us not overlook the ministry of Barnabas to John Mark. John Mark was the very subject of the disagreement between Paul and Barnabas, who having bailed out of his first missionary experience, was eventually restored to a position of affection to Paul. Paul specifically mentioned John Mark with positive terms in 2 Timothy 4:11, "Pick up Mark and bring him with you, for he is useful to me for service." God also blessed Barnabas' vision of rescuing and restoring John Mark, reestablishing him as an effective member of the missionary team.

James and Jude were sons of Mary and Joseph, and half-brothers of the Lord (God was the Father of our Lord Jesus). They resisted who Jesus was, perhaps were even a bit jealous, but later became disciples and authors of significant scriptural epistles.

Even Judas, the betrayer, was given a chance to turn from his evil betrayal. With the dipping of the bread into the bowl at the Passover supper, Jesus extended to Judas an expression of affection and the second chance to turn away from the horrendous sin he was about to commit.

---

[11] The Corinthian letters are actually letters two and four to that church. The first letter is referenced in 1 Corinthians 5:9. The third letter is referenced in 2 Corinthians 2:3. Also, Colossians 4:16 references a letter to the Laodiceans that was instructed to be read in the Colossian church.

What about us? Not one of us is without failure. Some of our failures are more private – impure thoughts, greed, the desire for things that God in His sovereignty has not given us (what the Bible calls covetousness), while others have externally visible failures, some of which may be monumental. Regardless of the category, all failures are painful to us and grievous to God. Not only is He pained by our pain, but our failures tarnish His reputation that we carry as people who bear His name (a truth most people seldom consider). Even after all our failures, God is gracious and merciful and His patience is extended toward us as objects of His mercy. God offers man repeated chances to return to that more abundant, more intimate relationship with Himself.

Repentance Brings More Light

Pause with me for a moment and notice something very significant about the sequence here. God waited for Jonah's repentance before giving a fresh word to him. You're probably familiar with the scenario, because just like Jonah, we've all been there many times. God gave us divine direction – a clear word – and we did something other than what He said. Like Jonah, we ran the other direction. We fell asleep in our spiritual responsibilities toward the people to whom God called us to give the Gospel. Some of us were even like Jonah in that, although our hearts were distant from God, we maintained the outward appearance of our religion, and all the while it was mere lip-service to following God because our hearts were askew; we were in the midst of self-willed behavior (rebellion) against Him. With some of us, we may have even reached the ultimate point of our heart's stumbling – preferring death to turning away from our rebellion.

Then came God's loving hand of discipline and we returned. We repented and returned to God because that is the nature of a genuine child of God. It was then that we were able to hear God's voice speaking to us afresh. It was a welcome word of mercy that the Father sent. In a blessed second chance, God said: *Go and fulfill My will and be blessed of your Father.*

Your Second Chance

How do you know if God will give you a second chance? What if you feel you're too far gone? Let me let you in on something. When you consider God's track record throughout Scripture, how long-suffering and kind He consistently shows Himself to be, there is no one too far from Him to return to His graces. To put it another way, as long as you are still alive and breathing earthly air, God is giving you a chance to come back and walk the straight and narrow way, to hold on to His divine hand (as it were), and to experience afresh the power that is His to deliver you from your sin, its tyranny, and its damaging effects. God is merciful to extend His gracious hand to you again. But there is a response from you that is expected and necessary. Getting a second chance from God will mean you will need to do certain things commensurate with obedience.

First, responding to God's second chance means *making a decision*. God said to Jonah, "Arise." To arise is to change your position, to move from sleep to wakefulness, from lethargy to action. To arise is to become conscious of a new day, a day of obedience, a day of walking with God, a day of hearing from His Word and determining to walk in submission to His life-giving Spirit so that *your* life may be the light of hope that the people around you need to see.

When we think about God's patience and mercy, it is obvious that enough time has passed for living in self-indulgence. We've spent enough time wallowing in the mire of self-pity. We may often want someone else to pick us up, but God says to every soul that is being offered His merciful second chance, *Wake up. Arise.*

Change your position. Enough is enough. Its time to decide to get on with what I've called you to do.

Secondly, after deciding to respond to God's invitation to obey, you will need to *decide on a course of action*. Getting a second chance from God means that action is required. God said to Jonah: "Go to Nineveh." When God, in His incredible and vast mercy, gives you a second chance, it requires action. Go! Be about your Father's business! Take up the duty from which you once left off. John the Baptist was perfectly in line with God's expectations when he preached to the people, "Bring forth fruits in keeping with your repentance" (cf. Matthew 3:8). Jonah's three-day undersea adventure had produced a renewed vigor for obeying God. Genuine repentance *always* produces obedience, and the renewed condition of your heart will be evidenced by obedience to God.

Thirdly, *return to the basics*. Getting a second chance from God will mean that you must do what God told you to do in the first place – proclaim God's message. God told Jonah to "Go to Nineveh and preach to it the message that I tell you." The instruction was a clear one, and the same one that God gave initially. Proclaim the word of the Lord as you received it.

This point cannot be overstressed. Our day is a day of multitudes of voices, opinions, and influences. Our culture is filled with learned voices to inform us of the latest study. Myriad books inundate us with self-help, human remedies for ailments that may even claim to deal with root issues. But root issues—issues of the heart—can only be cured with a divine touch, the Word from God as revealed in the Holy Scriptures and obedience to that Word.

The propensity of people these days is to go from counselor to counselor to find the "help" they need (I'm reminded of what the

Old Testament calls building cisterns that cannot hold water), while the Bible – the fountain of living waters – is left untouched, unopened, unread, and unproven. I am not advocating dismissing all counselors, for many do a wonderful service to Christ's people in bringing straying souls back to God. But what I wish we saw more is a return to the primacy of seeking God in His Word first and foremost! After all, does not Isaiah call Him the "Wonderful Counselor" (cf. Isaiah 9:6)?

The lesson of Jonah's second chance is a lesson each of us should allow to sink down deeply into the core of our beings. Your culture, your communities, your friends, your co-workers, and your family members need to hear a word from God. "Go and preach the message the I will tell you." You and I are the delivery persons for God's message. We are the spokespersons for the gospel of Jesus Christ! We are the ones to whom God has said, "Arise, go to Nineveh."

Our *Nineveh*, dear people of God, is the lost people around us. Who are they that are around us every day that know not the Savior? Who is it of our families who will spend eternity in the lake of fire unless they come in faith to Christ, their only hope? Who is it that we have convinced ourselves would never be interested in the gospel of Christ, when God has promised in John 12:32 that "If the Son of Man be lifted up, He will draw all men to Himself." Dear ones, will we believe God and proclaim the word that He has spoken, or will we continue in unbelief and disobedience?

The people of our day are accustomed to hearing weak words of men – opinions, studies, and surveys – but what they so desperately need is the sure word of God, spoken from the heart of God's servants who are confident in God's life-changing message. "Go and preach the message that I will tell you." As believers, God has saved us with the message of forgiveness and eternal life in Jesus Christ. That message ought to permeate our entire being. The Word of God residing in our hearts ought to naturally exude from our mouths in a joyful testimony of God's grace. Each of us should express the same level of confidence as did the apostle Paul (see Romans 1:16) when he said, "I am not ashamed of the gospel of Christ, for it is the power of God unto salvation to everyone who believes."

And finally, to take the second chance God offers we must *count the costs to us personally*. Experiencing the mercy of God in a second chance means that time and energy will be required of us. Notice Jonah 3:3, "Now Nineveh was an exceedingly great city, a three-day journey in extent. Jonah began to enter the city on the first day's walk." Although not specifically stated, the implication here is that Jonah spent at least 3 days preaching in the city.

Obedience is rarely convenient, and honestly, the inconvenience of obedience provides fodder for our heart's resistance. I wish I could tell you that I'm different or even that I have obtained a consistent victory. I haven't made it to perfection yet. We're all made of the same stuff. All of us are still in our flesh (that base and human part of us that still wants its own way, even though we are saved people). Our flesh wants to be placated. It seeks to justify itself way too easily. It finds ways to remain comfortable in its disobedience. This resistance is part of the spiritual conflict that goes on in the heart of a redeemed person (consider Paul's struggle revealed in Romans 7:7-25).

It is very uncomfortable to confront people with the Bible's teaching on the divine condemnation that all people inherit simply by being descendants of Adam. That is, however, precisely the duty to which we are called. Because until they hear that they are condemned, the concept of the mercy of God is meaningless and cannot be appreciated. It was the president of the Bible college where I attended, Robertson McQuilken, who said more than once, "Until one has heard the fearful thunderings from Sinai, he cannot appreciate the sweet echoes of mercy from Calvary."

A second chance will require time and energy in your obedience. If we don't have time to invest in the lives of the people around us—our children, our friends, our co-workers, our family, our neighbors, or even our acquaintances—we have not understood the love of God and we certainly have not understood the purpose of our lives as children of God on earth. God has saved us by His grace through faith in Jesus Christ to make disciples. Disciples are made from lost people. Lost people are all around us in the world and they need to hear of Christ.

God's mercy is seen in that He gives His servants second chances. God's nature will not change. He is acting toward us the way He has acted in all of recorded history. The question is this: will we take the mercy He is extending to us and engage His will? He has spoken. What direction do we intend to go?

These observations from Jonah's life should cause us to examine our own lives before the all-seeing eyes of God. There is always hope for the child of God. But God wants us to deal properly with the issues that have hindered our obedience to Him. We should ask ourselves this question: Is there an issue or an area of my walk with God where I have departed from God's calling? Hearing from God in a second chance means that a decision will need to be made to return to God's will. It will mean making a change in our position from distance to nearness, from omission to submission. Then we need to act on our word from God. If we have truly repented, our actions will show it. The return to God's will is the basic calling that is upon every believer's life –

to proclaim to the lost the way of salvation through Jesus Christ alone. Are we telling the lost around us that there is only one hope for their eternal life, and that hope is in Jesus Christ?

Finally, we must understand, embrace, and remember that there will be personal costs. You may find the path of obedience to be a lonely one. It will certainly cost us time and energy. Remember that our Lord Jesus, our example, left heaven to seek *us*. Why? Because heaven was boring and He needed something to occupy His time? Of course not. He came to seek and to save we who were lost. He perfectly understood our desperate condition, took pity on us and did something about the condemnation that was rightfully ours and the helplessness of our nature – our inability to get ourselves out of our own condemnation. Jesus spent three years training His disciples. He invested time and energy into His disciples, even enduring trouble and inconvenience in the process. He then commissioned them (and us) to take the good news of His gospel to every creature under heaven. That takes our time, our resources, our energies, and our efforts.

Ask yourself what you could do more than you are currently doing to witness to the lost around you. If you need assistance in technique or skills, ask your pastor or a trusted Christian friend to help you. There are many excellent resources in print that can also lend a hand. But whatever you do, do not remain the same in the light of God's merciful second chance toward you. If we are not willing to expend and be expended for God's kingdom, then we have not repented of our own selfish ways nor have we embraced His calling.

God is the God of the second chance. When He gives that second chance, we ought to run hard, fast, and gratefully back into His all-sufficiency in order to fulfill His will. Nothing else will bring the satisfaction of the intimate relationship with our Creator for which we were made.

Stumbling Toward Obedience

Depth of mercy can there be,
mercy still reserved for me?
Can my God His wrath forebear,
me the chief of sinners spare?

I have long withstood His grace,
long provoked Him to His face.
Would not harken to His call,
grieved Him by a thousand falls.

Now incline me to repent;
let me now my sins lament,
now my foul revolt deplore,
weep, believe, and sin no more.

There for me my Saviour stands,
holding forth His wounded hands;
God is love! I know, I feel,
Jesus weeps and loves me still.[12]

---

[12] Hymn. "Depth of Mercy." Charles Wesley. Public Domain

8

The God Who Pursues Sinners

Renewing Our View of God's Heart for the Lost

Jonah 3

At one time or another, every one of us has observed two people having a verbal "knock down, drag out." We may even have been part of it. Who wins? The one with the strongest argument, or the loudest, most persuasive voice? Perhaps the one who endures the longest or has the strongest, most stubborn will could be perceived as the winner.

God could win His argument with sinners with no effort whatsoever! He is the Supreme One of whom there is none greater. Yet He is never satisfied to simply have the upper hand over man, to wield His divine power over them unrivaled. God does not live to crush men under His feet, although He could with no effort whatsoever. God is not pleased to condemn; He desires to redeem. God's heart is to rescue, to free people from the condemnation of sin, and to receive penitent sinners into the relationship for which they were originally created. It is essential to understand, however, that those whom He receives, He first *pursues*.

There is probably no greater example of God's incredible pursuit of man in all of Scripture than the record of His pursuit of the Ninevites in the book of Jonah. Not only were these people lost and unreligious (a nice way of saying they were very evil people), they were content to live this way and nothing about them or their consciences was desirous of seeking God. In fact, there is no indication that they thought at all about the God of Israel, not even slightly.

Lost people are lost precisely because they have no ability to find their way out of their debacle, hence requiring someone else to find them. *God* is that someone else. He always takes the initiative with sinners. God pursues man because only He can. Only He has sufficient compassionate tenacity with which to pursue sinners. And God's tenacity is guided by His sovereign omnipotent and omniscient hand.

God pursues lost people because salvation was His idea. He is its divine author, its means, and its glorious object of praise. The way of salvation proceeded from His heart, it was revealed by His will, and He demonstrates His mercy and grace every time a sinner repents. He does not change, and the way He has acted in the past is precisely the way He will always act throughout all time and beyond.

God Always Sends a Person

God pursues man by sending a man. He always does. God sent Jonah, a person knowledgeable of the way of salvation, in order to proclaim to the Ninevites their only hope of averting disaster. In like manner, God has sent us to the lost around us. Jesus said, "As the Father has sent Me into the world, so send I you" (John

20:21). He also said, "You shall be my witnesses after the Holy Spirit has come upon you" (Acts 1:8).

If God's plan is to send people to proclaim to people, and God's Spirit is *in* the world, residing there through His people, why aren't we seeing more lost people converted to Christ? This is a perplexing question and one for which we shall seek an answer. Most of us live our everyday lives surrounded by people who need the Lord. And yet it is more and more difficult to see genuine conversions. Has the Lord changed in His approach to save the lost? Is His strength sapped by something more powerful? Is His hand slack or impotent to save? Of course not. How foolish!

The answer to our questions is simply this, that *we* are not going to our *Nineveh*. God's unchanging nature means that what He was in the Old Testament, He is also in the New. Nothing has changed about His character and His calling. His design is for redeemed man to bring to the ears of unredeemed man the message of hope in God through Christ's sacrifice of Himself in behalf of humanity. The startling reality that we all need to see is this: *we* are the "Jonahs" of our day. *We* are the ones God has sent – the ones through whom He pursues the lost.

We who have heard a clear word from God, are we obeying, or have we gone in a different direction? God has called us to go to the lost around us, but we often thoughtlessly or callously end up going in a direction different from God's call. We board the ships of material pursuits. We pay the fare for the position for which we long. We sell out for prestige, relational security, or daily routines that do not include God's agenda. We often assume life as usual, when the judgment coming to lost people is anything but usual.

God is still pursuing man. We may not be engaging His purposes nor living in strict obedience to His calling, but that doesn't change the calling of God upon our lives. Like Jonah, God's call to us remains. Yet, even when we live disobediently to God's call, we are still the objects of His mercies and are being given multiple chances to obey His call.

In Romans 10:14, Paul employs logic to help us see the plight of the lost from their point of view. "How shall they call on Him in whom they have not believed? And how shall they believe in Him of whom they have not heard? And how shall they hear without a preacher?" Beloved ones, God pursues lost people and He does so by sending His own children—those who have experienced His love and forgiveness—to proclaim the way of averting eternal disaster and instead, receiving eternal life.

God loves to save sinners. That is the story of the Bible and it is the story of His intervention in man's history. The Ninevites were under God's just condemnation for their wickedness and were objects of His righteous wrath. But in that state, they were also objects of God's love and mercy.

What Genuine Repentance Looks Like

Look at how the Ninevites' change of heart began. First, they entered into a relationship with the almighty and merciful God through repentance. Their repentance began when they believed the Word of God. What refreshing words we read in chapter 3, verse 5, "So the people of Nineveh believed God." Jonah preached to them the judgment to come and they believed what God said. That's the beginning of genuine repentance.

Second, verses 5 and 6 indicate that their repentance was demonstrated through humility.

> So the people of Nineveh believed God, proclaimed a fast, and put on sackcloth, from the greatest to the least of them. Then word came to the king of Nineveh; and he

arose from his throne and laid aside his robe, covered *himself* with sackcloth and sat in ashes.

They were so deeply disturbed over the message of their offense to God, that their daily routines were affected. They proclaimed a fast and they put on sackcloth. Both of these actions were an outward demonstration of the humility of the heart; they wanted everyone who saw them to not only know, but to join them in humbling their hearts before an angered almighty deity.

Thirdly, they had a sense of urgency to act. True Holy Spirit conviction of sin brings with it an urgency to flee from the wrath to come. To do otherwise is not to repent but only to give lip service to repentance. But I should remind you that lip service is insufficient to save. Only a posture of being poor in spirit – a humility that invokes an urgency to fall on the mercies of God – is the posture of salvation.

Resultantly, they experienced a prevailing fear of God. The outward demonstrations of the inward repentance were widespread, and it is safe to say that a fear of God fell upon the city of Nineveh. Their actions perfectly demonstrated the truth James wrote when he said, "As the body without the spirit is dead, so faith without works is dead also" (cf. James 2:26).

In light of our day's wide spread attitude of nonchalance toward God and the conformity to holiness that the Bible teaches ought to accompany genuine conversion, it should be soberly considered here that if we are not afraid of God's judgment, we will not flee from our own wickedness. Depravity is too deep and too ingrained in the human heart. Certainly if the Ninevites had not been afraid of God, they would have changed nothing. But the account shows that they, in fact, changed *everything*.

In response to their repentance, what did God say? *OK, I've got you now, you dirty rotten sinners. Now I can destroy you like I've wanted to for all these years.* Hardly! God recognized their genuine repentance. "God saw their works that they turned from their evil way" (Jonah 3:10). God saw! He always sees. He's looking for hearts that are penitent and that understand the criterion for coming to Him. Second Chronicles 16:9 reminds us, "The eyes of the Lord run to and fro throughout the earth, seeking someone whose heart is completely His, to show Himself strong in their behalf."

God saw their works, *that they turned from their evil.* They brought forth works in keeping with their repentance. Not works in order to achieve salvation, but works that evidence true salvation being present and genuine.

If you say you've repented, but keep doing the same sins unabated, the sobering reality is that you haven't repented. Repentance is more than feeling badly about what we are or what we've done. Genuine repentance is a decision to change. God saw the reality of their heart repentance as it was demonstrated in their behavior.

Judgment Averted

As a result of what they did, God relented concerning their impending judgment. To relent does not mean that God changed His mind. God did not change His mind. His character is unchanging and as such, He perpetually exists in a posture of mercy toward sinners who repent. So when God "relented" of His judgment against the Ninevites, it was in absolute agreement with His divine character – all His attributes existing harmoniously together in perfection. To relent is better understood to mean: to take a softer approach. And God did exactly that. Like the equitable and benevolent Father that He is, once His warning had been heeded, He took a softer approach. He did not bring upon them the predicted disaster. This is the nature of our God. He pursues sinners and forgives those who repent.

Messengers of Hope

God is a God of incredible mercy. He has demonstrated His mercy in providing a second chance to an erring servant and in receiving sinners who repented. You should be aware, however, that God's mercy is not limitless. There is a judgment coming. For now, God withholds His judgment in order to be merciful so that men will flee from the wrath to come and into His arms of mercy. Nor is God's mercy purposeless. When God extends His mercy, it is to invoke a response of obedience from the objects of His mercy.

God pursued the Ninevites and He pursued the prophet who was to bring them a message of hope. Both were the objects of His mercy, but the Ninevites could only repent if God's servant obediently gave God's message. We too are God's messengers of hope, and whenever we discover that we have forsaken the path of proclaiming salvation to the lost around us, we must make a decision to change our ways. Genuine repentance will always mean that our behavior will be in keeping with our decision.

O precious people, speak the word of God to lost people. Understand that obedience requires your time and energy. Remember also that God pursues sinners in order to receive them when they repent. As Ezekiel 18:32 so poignantly reminds us, "He takes no pleasure in the death of the wicked."

Some reading this book will need to respond to God's pursuit of *you* today. God is still giving you breath and life, therefore He is still pursuing you. Moses said, "Here I set before you this day life and death, blessing and cursing; therefore choose life" (Deuteronomy 30:19).

Remember that God pursues sinners in order to receive them when they repent. There is a Nineveh all around us. That means that it is open season on lost people. God's commands are clear;

His mercy is sure, but it is not limitless. It will someday be eclipsed by His justice on that great day of reckoning. The grace of God that saves sinners is also on a time table. It is not only the time table of the cosmos, but also of the limited number of people's days on earth. Compared to eternity, a person's lifespan is a very narrow window in which decisions for eternity are made. Once life is over, the eternal destiny of the soul is irrevocable and unable to be changed. The saved will spend eternity in the blessedness of heaven with their Lord and enjoying His glorious presence, but the lost will spend eternity in the fire that is never quenched.

If you have been negligent or thoughtless or perhaps even rebellious in your spiritual duties, decide today to be about your Father's business. There is no greater joy than laying down your own life, only to have God fill it with the life and resurrection power of His Son, who was the embodiment on earth of the mercy of God toward man.

If you are in need of God's mercy on *your* soul, take a moment right now to be alone with Him, confess what you've come to realize about yourself, and ask Him to place you once again on the pathway to obedience to His call. Paul's reminder to a first century church (First Thessalonians 5:24) is pertinent for us as well. "Faithful is He who calls you, and He also will bring it to pass."

9
The Sins of a Stumbling Heart

Recognizing the Sins that Hinder Obedience to God's Call

Jonah 4

I remember the first time I looked at something under a microscope. It was totally fascinating to see one-celled microorganisms swimming around in a drop of pond water. Later in high school biology, one of my favorite parts of class was the lab, where I could view differing kinds of cells, observing the amazing details of their composition. I felt privileged to see with the microscope what was not apparent to the naked eye.

In a similar way, that is what God has done in chapter four from the scriptural account of Jonah's personal testimony. He has given us His written revelation as the instrument for seeing what we could not otherwise see on our own. And thus, we have occasion to peer down into the spiritual molecular makeup of the heart (as it were) of this most imperfect servant of God.

Romans 15:4 affirms that "the things that were written before were written for our leaning, that we through patience and encouragement of the Scriptures might have hope." So let us look carefully at this account which offers a revealing view of the heart of the prophet – that which incited him to rebel in the first place, and that which continued to give him difficulty, even in the midst of his obedience. Indeed, this accounts for his imperfect obedience, even after his repentance, as well as his wavering faith in God.

As children, you learned in your Sunday schools the story of Jonah's flight from God, and you understood the thrust of this book: his call from God to preach to Nineveh, his running from God, his repentance in the belly of the fish, and his eventual obedience. But did you know that the book also takes a plunge into the depths of his heart? The revelations of Jonah's heart issues reveal the root of his floundering obedience. And that is what I want to focus on here – that dark part of our hearts that keeps us from walking in the Word of God.

A Common Struggle

Jonah is not the only servant of God to have this struggle. Indeed, we all do! Listen to Paul's inner struggle revealed in Romans 7.

> 15. For what I am doing, I do not understand. For what I will to do, that I do not practice; but what I hate, that I do.
> 16. If, then, I do what I will not to do, I agree with the Law that it is good.
> 17. But now, it is no longer I who do it, but sin that dwells in me.
> 18. For I know that in me (that is, in my flesh) nothing good dwells; for to will is present with me, but how to perform what is good I do not find.
> 19. For the good that I will to do, I do not do; but the evil that I will not to do, that I practice.

As we read those words, many of us were screaming inside, *Yes, yes, that's me.* So why don't we walk in the way of the Lord more consistently? Why don't we keep the ways of God in obedience to the same level that we understand them? Why is there often a disconnect between what we *know* and what we *do*?

Some of God's people (could one of them be you?) are in deep, deep heart trouble today. You may be entertaining thoughts that are foreign to your confession as a believer in Jesus Christ. You may have picked up this book because you sensed your own sin-laden pursuit of God and your hard-heartedness at times. You have Christ in you, the hope of glory, and yet you find yourself at times as temporal minded as any unbeliever on the street. You are a part of the church, the body of Christ, saved people with a common bond in the power and hope of our resurrected Lord Jesus Christ, and yet you feel isolated and lonely in your heart's need. You have the living Truth residing within your heart, but you, more often than not, embrace the shallow and errant philosophies of the world without even slowing down to evaluate whether or not they are true or false, helpful or harmful in your walk with God.

I have met scores of people who claim to be followers of Jesus Christ, and yet they walk in confusion, never coming to terms with who they are in Christ, never coming to understand and embrace His purposes for their lives on earth. Resultantly, as someone once said, they have just enough Christianity to make them miserable, but not enough to bring them joy. Can anyone identify with that predicament?

I believe the testimony of Jonah's life will help us uncover the stumbling blocks in our own walks with God. For those of us who are sick of our ailing flesh consistently getting the best of us, there is good news. God will equip us for a more holy, more successful life of service unto Him as we give heed to His Word.

Peering Deeply into Jonah's Heart

God's call was on Jonah's life, and because he was a genuine child of God his disobedience invoked the discipline of God in his life. Being in a state of heart that causes a man to flee from God's presence is a state that requires God's severe intervention. By the way, God's discipline does not usually include plush accommodations, and I cannot imagine any more undesirable accommodations than Jonah's.

Jonah had repented in the midst of discipline and subsequently obeyed the Word of the Lord by proclaiming to Nineveh their impending judgment. Because of their repentance, God turned from His anger toward Nineveh. But oddly, Jonah became angry. This is a very strange reaction for a preacher to have when people respond to his preaching in repentance.

Why was Jonah angry? What was wrong with his heart that he would respond to God's mercy toward sinners in such an ungodly way? Even though he outwardly walked in obedience, his heart was still very needy (much like many of us). His sins were subtle, and as such, they were all the more deceitful and difficult to deal with. We will look at what chapter 4 reveals as Jonah's sins.

Prejudice

Proclaiming God's message to lost people assumes God's heart of compassion toward them, so that when they repent God will receive them. Conversely, Jonah's perspective toward the people of Nineveh is anything but compassionate. His judgmental attitude against the people God sought to save reveals a prejudicial spirit deep inside of him. From his point of view, they were not God's chosen people and he was not happy about them being spared from judgment. Jonah had never come to understand God's heart for lost people, that it is not His will that any should perish, and he, therefore, conducted himself in a superior manner with a prejudicial look toward outsiders. Prejudice finds a fertile breeding ground in an attitude of superiority. In Jonah's case, he was called to preach the Word of God to a people that God always intended for Israel to reach with the message of His salvation.

I find it amazing how the sin of prejudice can so easily (and even peacefully) coexist in people who profess to truly know Christ. Many of God's people have issues in the arena of prejudice. I have had opportunity to reside in several different sections of the United States. I have also dwelt and worked outside of our country. In every place I've lived, prejudice has surfaced in one form or another.

I grew up in the south where race relations have historically been newsworthy. Even with many decades of strides in the right direction, prejudice in the south today is alive and well. But it is not the fault of only one people group. Prejudice knows no one direction. Every race bears some guilt in its attitudes toward others.

Additionally, the last eight years of my ministry have been spent establishing Bible institutes in the Caribbean islands. These island nations are populated mostly by people of color, but even among *them,* prejudice toward one another is nearly electric. To island people, it does not seem sufficient to merely be of the negro race. The darker one's skin color, the more likely it is that he or she will be looked down upon. I have discovered this prejudicial tendency to be pervasive, and people I know in this circumstance substantiate this discovery. In the islands, prejudice enjoys an appalling level of normalcy.

The first time this was explained to us, my wife and I were at lunch with new friends in a remote island of the western Caribbean. Our friends are dark in their skin color. As they explained to us the prevailing situation of racial discrimination, we were astounded. "But we are very dark," our friend continued, "and therefore we are low in the social structure. But because some have seen us here today with you, our new white friends, we have possibly been bumped up on the ladder of social status." Our astonishment went sky high.

Let me give you a more humorous example of prejudice that we've noticed while ministering in the Caribbean. We are often among a very few number of white people in a congregation on Sunday mornings. In fact, sometimes we are the only ones. We have noticed in the Caribbean that when a black preacher tells a story involving a white man, he often feels compelled to identify the man in the story as *white*. The reverse happens in the southern United States, only with the same point. Often a white person telling a story involving a man of color seems compelled to identify the person in the story as a *black* man.

Why do people act this way toward other races, especially when the color of a person is almost always irrelevant and inconsequential to the story? I believe it is because racial prejudice lurks just below the surface of society, seeking to exalt self by lowering others. At times this may even exist within those who suppose an unprejudiced social outlook. You may balk at that conclusion, but may I ask you, *what difference does it make to a story what color a person is?* A man is a man, made in the image of God. So this little question can also become a test as to whether or not our hearts are subtly exalting themselves over others. Do we feel compelled to speak of other races in a way that lowers them and elevates ourselves, even subtly? If so, racial prejudice probably exists within us. Jonah had to understand his problem with prejudice and many of us still need to come to terms with it ourselves. Because if there is an attitude of superiority or the tendency to look down on others, our hearts might very well be insensitive to that other person's need for the gospel of Jesus Christ.

A Distorted View of God

Jonah also possessed a skewed view of God. Jonah's society was a prosperous one. The Bible places his ministry during the time of Jeroboam II of the northern kingdom of Israel, roughly 931 – 910 BC. History records life under Jeroboam II as one that enjoyed a prosperous economy, world influence, and luxurious living. Because life in the northern kingdom of Israel was good, the prevailing opinion about the nation was that its financial solvency and prosperity were evidences that she enjoyed the blessing of God. Their assumed formula for success went something like this: *a good economy plus material prosperity equals God's blessing.*

On top of all this, this period was preceded by a supposed religious awakening. Jeroboam II's grandfather, King Jehu, was God's instrument for ridding the country of Ahab and Jezebel's wickedness. And while the blessing of positive political change was a real one, it came despite the absence of genuine spiritual awakening, not because of it. The reality was that of dualism: that in the midst of a nationally pervasive religious expression, personal wickedness abounded.

Within the framework of this dualistic society, and because it was rooted in a distorted view of God, it was easy to develop a superior attitude regarding oneself and an unfavorable, even derisive, attitude toward others. God's favor was certainly demonstrated toward His people, but it was because of His nature of goodness and not because of their godly behavior. They simply were not godly.

It is imperative for God's children, as those called to follow His word, to maintain a biblical perspective on our world, and to not substitute it for a more popular one. The world system, our flesh, and our enemy the devil, all constantly bombard us with false philosophy, worldly intrusion, and sinful indulgences. We must devote ourselves unswervingly to reprogramming our minds with God's Word on a daily basis or we will likewise succumb to a distorted view of God. God calls all His children into a relationship of communion and intimacy with Himself. To know Him intimately is to follow His word. To follow His Word, one must first *know* His Word. Jesus said (John 14:15), "If you love Me, you will keep My commands."

Think of knowing and using God's Word like seeing life through a filtered lens—the filter of revealed truth. It is through this filtered lens that life is to be interpreted. When we have the wrong filter (some value system other than God's revealed truth), we will have the tendency to misinterpret events, people, and circumstances. Jesus communicated this same idea like this,

> The lamp of the body is the eye. If therefore your eye is good, your whole body will be full of light. But if your eye is bad, your whole body will be full of darkness. If therefore the light that is in you is darkness, how great is that darkness!"
>
> —Matthew 6:22-23

Jesus is speaking of the process of coming to *understand*. The eye He speaks of is the window of the mind, our power to observe. What results from the observation is either enlightenment or darkening, depending on how we interpret what we observe. Notice, though, the problem of making wrong observations: "If the light that is in you is darkness." This is figurative language meaning that your interpretation of life is found to be flawed. You view it as light—a right perspective, illumination. In reality, though, it is darkness and a failure to see properly or understand accurately. Such a skewed perspective will surely lead to misinterpreting events, circumstances, people, and (could it be?) even the words of Scripture.

Jonah lost his perspective on the lost people of his day. Many of us may have lost perspective as well. When God's perspective has been eclipsed by a lesser, more self-centered one, our worldview becomes faulty. With a distorted view of God and its resulting jaded worldview, open doors to proclaim the gospel to the lost it might very well be viewed, not as the priority of life that they should be, but as interruptions to our busy schedules or inconveniences to our daily routines.

Anger with God

When we couple the problem of a distorted view of God with a God-given guilt over disobeying His commands, (guilt we do not often recognize because of our heart condition) then emotions toward God can arise that should not be. Jonah 4:1 says, "It displeased Jonah, and he became angry." The Hebrew is much stronger here, literally *"It was evil to Jonah,* and he became angry." It vexed Jonah to the core of his being. It irritated him that God turned from His wrath against the people of Nineveh. Why? Because even though he was disciplined and eventually did fulfill his calling to preach repentance to them, he still obeyed with a heart that was impure with resident sins that were not fully surrendered. The sad truth is that he didn't want the Ninevites to repent. He wanted them to die for their wickedness. Jonah actually wanted God to kill them for their evil ways, not show mercy on them.

What an amazing contradiction in the heart of God's servant. He who had received God's mercy in himself wanted people—the very people God sent him to rescue—to experience God's destructive wrath. Jonah's distorted view of God caused him to focus on the part of God's character that *he* wanted expressed (wrath), while ignoring the part of God's character that moves Him to pursue man, seek his repentance and to offer him pardon (mercy). For Jonah, the circumstances of his calling had turned out differently than he expected, and that made him angry. Jonah's anger was aimed at God, to be sure. It became apparent that God was not following Jonah's agenda, and this made him angry.

As followers of Jesus Christ we must ask ourselves a hard question. How deeply does anger hold onto us? Related to this question, and serving in some ways as its remedy, have we spent enough time in God's Word to understand His heart and His ways for the lost?

People become angry because they have not gotten their way over something in life or in the church. They stew in a distorted, irritable misery and life eventually becomes toxic. As their lives go on, they become more and more edgy, which is a nice way of saying they have become more controlled by anger. Much of the time the disposition of their hearts remains a mystery even to themselves because of their sustained absence from and avoidance of God's Word. However, as James 1:22-25 instructs us, God's Word acts as a mirror to our hearts to reveal what we're truly like. Instead of reading God's Word and responding to its revelation of the heart, anger is often covered up with skilled exercises in superficiality—friendliness, incessant talking, or efforts at being the funniest person in social circles. Some people even allow their coddled anger to develop into a victim mentality, convincing themselves (accompanied by efforts to convince those around them as well) that they are not to blame; others are.

All of these maladies hide our true depth of depravity in adversarial attitudes toward God. But God is not fooled. And the message of this book is that God will deal with those renegade attitudes. The question is, when He does deal with them, will you have so convinced yourself of a psychological malady or a victim status, that you will not be able to hear the voice of God?

I want to make a statement here that you may have to think about for a while. If you don't understand it at first, pause and reflect on the previous paragraph and this statement regarding man's anger. Put on your theological seatbelt and brace yourself to read my assertion. Here it is. If God is sovereign over all of life (like the Bible teaches us that He is), then all human anger is directed ultimately at God and His sovereign rule over us. Read that last sentence over again if you need to, because it's true. And the outworking of internal anger at God is: fault-finding, complaining, bitterness, resentment, and ingratitude. Anger can even culminate in feelings of purposelessness in following God, that continuing this Christian life is little more than a waste of time. If any of these symptoms are yours, then it is highly likely that your heart has an anger issue with God.

Jonah's skewed perspective of God and his resulting anger caused a heart shift. He was no longer guided by the will of God, but by another manifestation of his wayward heart, one that often resides in the human heart unchallenged—self-centeredness.

Self-Centeredness

> So he prayed to the Lord, and said, "Ah, Lord, was not this what I said when I was still in my country? Therefore I fled to Tarshish; for I know that You are a gracious God, slow to anger and abundant in lovingkindness, One who relents from doing harm. Therefore now, O Lord, please take my life from me, for it is better for me to die than to live!
>
> —Jonah 4:2,3

Jonah's attitude toward God in this statement implicates his imbalanced concern for his own reputation. He knew God would turn from His wrath if the Ninevites repented. They did repent, and afterward Jonah probably felt like a fool for proclaiming destruction toward them. If he rejoiced in the nature of God (His goodness, mercy and grace toward sinners), the Ninevites' repentance would have ushered in great joy of heart for the prophet. Jonah's reaction, on the other hand, was anger because they repented. His own reputation, in light of his most recent sermon proclaiming imminent destruction, seemed to be more important to him than the mercy of God toward people in danger of His wrath.

Have you been disappointed or hurt by others? Have you ever wanted divine justice on them? And yet when it didn't come, did you became angry and embittered in your hearts? Be honest. If you answered positively, you have something else to think about. You may think that you're angry at the people involved, but in reality this anger and bitterness is toward God who, in unchallenged sovereignty, rules over all things in the universe, including all the details of *your life*. Indeed, He rules over all our lives.

This is a point in our study where we should pause and remind ourselves of the Bible's teaching concerning our merits; that not even the best of us is deserving of God's mercy. All our righteousness before God is as a filthy garment in comparison with God's absolute holiness. All of us are deserving of the full expression of His wrath. God would be just if He condemned us all to the fires of hell for all of eternity. And in doing so, not one iota of His holy character would suffer the slightest stain because the execution of His wrath would be done in harmony with His perfect nature. Yet God seeks the salvation of the lost. While His heart is grieved and angered by man's rebellion, He is also moved to a compassionate posture toward man that causes the expression of His wrath to be eclipsed by His mercy toward fallen creatures.

So with that said, why would anyone consider it a reason to be angry that God would have mercy on our enemies, just like He had mercy on *us* when *we* were His enemies? Because our hearts have the idol of *themselves,* and it is *ourselves* that we serve. This is a sin (like all sins) that requires recognition and then repentance. Jonah, however, sank even further downward.

A Haughty Spirit

> Then the Lord said, "Is it right for you to be angry?"
> So Jonah went out of the city and sat on the east side of the city.
>
> —Jonah 4:4,5

Notice that Jonah did not answer God's question in verse 4, but like a spoiled child he stomped out of the city to see if something catastrophic would happen. A haughty spirit is evidenced by reactionary tendencies couched in a refusal to listen to God's Word—either actively or passively. Active reactions are verbal or behavioral rejection of God's corrective confrontations. A passive reaction is indecision or avoiding an action we know we should do.

Divine confrontation may come from the Holy Spirit as He produces legitimate guilt in us for wrong actions or attitudes. It may come when a fellow Christian lovingly confronts us concerning our spiritual condition or directly by the Spirit of God as He confronts our errant condition through His Word. No matter how He does it and no matter from what source the confrontation comes, we have two choices—we can either turn from sin by responding to God's confrontation or we can continue downward into a further self-destruction of the heart. Jonah chose the latter.

Unbelief

> "till he might see what would become of the city."
>
> —Jonah 4:5

Hello, Jonah! God just turned away from His wrath. What are you doing wondering what will become of the city? Not only is this pure unbelief, but in his warped thinking, his angrily selfish orientation, and his haughty spirit, he had completely discarded the truth about God that he knew, that God was a God of mercy toward all who repent. That's what unbelief does. It first becomes hardened to the truth, then it discards God's Word in favor of our own word or the word of some other erroneous perspective.

The indications of Jonah's unbelief were a sadistic joy at the potential judgment of others, and an overwhelmingly negative perspective on life. His sadistic thinking evidenced itself in that he awaited Nineveh's destruction. His negative outlook displayed itself as he said absolutely nothing positive during God's confrontation of his heart's condition.

Have you ever known someone like that? The world would prescribe the remedy to this person's condition as a need to make efforts at being more positive. But the true need of the heart is to recognize his rejection of the Word of God. Unbelief is remedied by repentance, not positive thinking. True repentance releases one's will and desire to the control of God for His purposes, embracing what God says in all its purity and simplicity. If this is not done, the heart will descend further downward, as did Jonah's.

Despair

> And it happened, when the sun arose, that God prepared a vehement east wind; and the sun beat on Jonah's head, so that he grew faint. Then he wished death for himself, and said, "It is better for me to die than to live."
>
> —Jonah 4:8

Jonah's despair grew out of physical exhaustion: "He grew faint." He responded inappropriately to God's chastening: "He wished death for himself." And he despaired of life: "and said, 'It is better for me to die than to live.'" And that disparity produced the further skewed perspective of irrationality.

Irrationality

> "It is right for me to be angry, even to death!"
>
> —Jonah 4:9

Have you ever tried to talk sense to an angry, depressed, and irrational person? As Vance Havner once said, you may as well try to "catch rays of sun with a fishhook." Jonah defended his right to be angry. But Jonah's anger is in stark contrast to the love and mercy of God being extended to the Ninevites. It is evident that Jonah's anger has absolutely no justification whatsoever. It is irrational.

Apart from a monumental intervention of God, irrationality leaves a person locked into his own perspective, unable to process logically. Our mental institutions are full of people in this category. Additionally, as a pastor I knew people who could no longer process God's truth rationally because of their consistent refusal to deal properly with issues that led to their present state of heart.

As we have seen, much heart destruction has preceded the indications about which I have written here. And all these heart issues in the man of God led to the final heart manifestation.

Stubbornness of Heart

> Then God said to Jonah, "Is it right for you to be angry about the plant?"
> And he said, "It is right for me to be angry, even to death!"
>
> —Jonah 4:9

Notice that Jonah's anger and skewed perspective led him into continuing on a course of sin in light of convincing evidence that he was wrong. His course of action should have been to repent immediately once God confronted his sin. Instead he choose to justify himself in the face of God's clear conviction from His Word.

A stubborn heart is a heart where sin has reached its full maturity. It is the condition of a believer's heart—once transformed, once devoted to pure and unhindered worship of God Almighty—but now has turned to its own anger, its own resentment, its own agenda, its own rationale, and its own ways. It is noteworthy that delayed obedience or passivity in regards to the need for obedience is equal to stubbornness of heart. This is a spiritual condition that is placed in an alarming light in 1 Samuel 15:23: "Stubbornness is as iniquity and idolatry."

God forbid that this should be the plight of anyone reading this book, but certainly there are some for whom this is God's intended message. Has God shined His holy light on a sinful area of your heart? What will you do with what you now know about your heart?

10
Ensuring Obedience has a Fighting Chance

It is never enough just to have our sins exposed, or to simply gain awareness of the problem. As Christians, we want to change. Change is God's goal as well – change into the image of Jesus Christ. So what is the solution for a heart that has become so entangled in sin that it cannot see the way out?

There were steps to Jonah's healing that, although not explicitly written out in his little book, are nonetheless inherent within his writing. Careful examination of his writing, as well as his style, reveal these steps to we who are seeking to learn from Jonah's example.

Honesty

Jonah had digressed to the edge of wishing for his own death. He was at the bottom of life, in the pit of despair as a servant of God. Yet, he is the Spirit-chosen author of this book. Jonah wrote about his own downward spiral with such brutal honesty that one can only admire him for his courage at self-revelation. Honesty in the midst of heart trouble is not only necessary, it is essential. We can, however, find ourselves fearful of being honest about what is going on within our own hearts. What if your own level of honesty scares you? What if being brutally honest means that you sound like an unbeliever, or one who has already fallen off the deep end?

First, realize that God already knows what you have just discovered about yourself. In fact, He has known it from eternity past. Furthermore, it was *Him* who showed *you* your true condition. This is God's mercy designed to draw the stumbling believer back into intimacy and fellowship with Himself. So realizing that you are now being honest is a very positive thing, even if the honesty itself has a very negative and distasteful flavor to it.

Even more important is to recognize that if there is the slightest twinge of honesty in the heart of a person who has sunk to these depths, it is precisely because the Spirit of God is still at work in his heart. God is working to heal and to return His erring child to a relationship He, the living God, created you to enjoy, a relationship of the Father with His child.

What if you have already stumbled? What if your heart has already begun manifesting characteristics of hardness or insensitivity to God? If you can see where you are in the process, you're not too far gone. In fact, if you respond honestly to God right now as He speaks to you in your trouble, you will discover yourself recognizing the accuracy of *His perspective* as revealed in His Word. And when you see that God was right to begin with, and that your own efforts at self-justification and escapism are useless, then you are on the brink of the repentance that will bring new freedom and growth to your heart.

Confession

Honesty about your true condition must yield confession. It does no good to see a problem if there is not a solution put into place. Confession of sin is the doorway through which we begin to return to God.

So what do we mean by "confessing our sins?" Confession is saying about your sin what God says about it. It is *agreeing with God* concerning what He already sees your sin to be and how He has revealed it to you. After honestly evaluating yourself, you are now ready to agree with God as He convicts you of the sins He has revealed to you.

How is this done? Consider Jonah's example. As we carefully examine Jonah's book, we see a man who throughout his writing bared his soul in honest and brutal self-revelation. His personal testimony of his waywardness as a servant of God is a telling confession of his sins before God's all-seeing eyes. Honesty of evaluation will yield the necessity of accurate confession – agreeing with God concerning our sins.

As new covenant believers, we have the New Testament for clarity in instruction. In 1 John 1:9 we read, "If we confess our sins, He is faithful and just to forgive us our sins and to cleanse us from all unrighteousness." The Greek term the apostle John used for *confess* is *homologeo*. It means literally *to say the same thing as*. Saying what God says about sin means not just admitting that we sinned, but expressing our transgression as that, a breaking of God's covenant and His standard of holiness. We should not simply say that we're sorry, but speak to our Father regarding the specific sin that has offended Him as the Lover of our souls and the One who redeemed us by the blood of His Son.

A puritan once wrote, "The heinousness of sin lies not so much in the nature of the sin committed as in the greatness of the One sinned against.[13] The One with whom we are in relationship is the One of whom none is greater. Therefore, any sin is an affront and an offense to the greatness of God's majestic Person. That alone should be enough to stop us in our tracks, but usually it is not. The sinfulness of our fleshly hearts is great and trespassing God's boundaries is an all-too-familiar state of our hearts. So we must exercise ourselves toward confession before the all-seeing eyes of our great God.

Within the heart of God is also an emotional element regarding our sinfulness. When we sin, our sins bring a measure of sorrow and injury to God's heart as well. Listen to Ezekiel 6:9, "I was crushed by their adulterous heart which has departed from Me, and by their eyes which play the harlot after their idols."

It is true that nothing can separate us from the love of God, but the relationship we enjoy with God must be cared for in love toward Him. Confessing our offense to the offended party (in this case, God) is an expression of love—love for Him who has borne our offenses over and over and not dealt with us according to our sins, but according to His great and vast mercy (see Psalm 103:10-11). This type of honest and revealing confession also expresses the value of our relationship with God, with the ultimate goal of restored fellowship. Specific confession (homolegeo: saying what God says about the offense) is confession that deals with the exact sin or sins that brought distortion to our relationship with God.

In addition to the specific sin itself that needs to be confessed, there is something else to consider. Have you ever realized that acts of sin bring other acts of sin with them—peripheral sins? For instance, in Ephesians, Paul gives believers commands like these: "walk in a manner worthy of the calling with which you were called" (4:1) and "be filled with the Spirit" (5:18). There are

---

[13] *The Valley of Vision, p. 143*. A Collection of Puritan Prayers and Devotions. Banner of Truth Trust, Carlisle, PA. 1975.

also other commands, but these will serve our purpose here as examples. Committing the sin of lust, for instance, is a violation of the command to walk worthy of the gospel, but it also violates the command to be filled with the Spirit (it is difficult to be under the control of the Holy Spirit while at the same time being lured and controlled by the flesh through lust). Additionally lust transgresses the marriage covenant. These peripheral sins need to be acknowledged and confessed as well.

Our duty is not to go on a sin hunt. This would not only be legalistic, but also exhausting and discouraging. On the contrary, we should simply respond to conviction that the Spirit of God brings into our hearts. He is the living God and one of His prime objectives is that we walk in truth before His all-seeing eyes. Therefore, all sin that the Spirit of God reveals to us should be confessed. I make it a practice in the confessions of my own sins to include my violations of God's related commands (like the ones mentioned above), simply because sin is rarely a matter of one issue. My desire in confession is to have the purity of communication in my relationship with my Father restored again (1 John 1:9), so communing with God regarding my offense toward Him and confessing according to all that the Holy Spirit reveals to me is what I need to do. When a stumbling of the heart achieves reality within us, it comes not only with the sin that is manifested and obvious, but also with less visible sins that feed the manifestation.

Lastly, agreeing with God means that the sins He has brought to our attention need to be forsaken. Proverbs 28:13 says: "He who covers his sins will not prosper, but whoever confesses and forsakes them will have mercy." God's ways are best and He instructs us accordingly because confession of sins returns us to a state of living where His greatest joy is now within reach of His broken and repentant child. Confession is the doorway back into intimacy with God.

Experiencing Renewal

Once we have honestly considered God's words, and have agreed with Him in prayerful confession and repentance, we will receive the blessing of being renewed by His presence. In his message on the Day of Pentecost, Peter said, "Repent...so that times of refreshment may come from the presence of the Lord" (Acts 3:19). Times of refreshment in repentance come when the soul is cleansed, when the "white flag" of surrender to God's will has been run up the flag pole of our hearts. Our hearts' tendency to flee from God's presence (cf. Jonah 1:3) is brought to a halt because it is precisely that Presence that has brought us to repentance and renewal. The soul that now walks in the light of God's revelation instead of the darkness of its own sinful perspective experiences life anew, much like awakening to a new day refreshed and renewed.

Being renewed and refreshed in God will rekindle a love for His presence, a desire for His conviction, and the warmth of His fatherly love that drove Him to discipline us for our sins. We will also desire His deepening intimate involvement in our lives as well as His commands and calling upon our lives as His chosen instruments for the gospel. God renews and refreshes the mind, the will, the heart and even the body of His repentant servants and gives us deepening desires to pursue Him further in order to maintain renewal and adherence to His will.

Reflection

Did you ever go through a difficult time and later look back and see how God was there in the midst of that difficulty? In the context of returning to an intimate relationship with God, the knowledge of His ever-abiding presence with you will be your cornerstone of hope. Reflection after confession and renewal allows us to see more clearly what we were unable to see in the midst of our sinful stumbling. Looking back on the matter with renewed eyes, we are able to see both the depth and the danger of unrestrained sin. This is insight we did not have while in a posture of running from God. God renews the minds of His repentant servants and quickens us to more clearly see His sovereignty over our lives.

And here is an amazing truth. He never stopped being sovereign over us and our circumstances. He never once slipped off the throne of the universe in absolute and unrivaled sovereignty, even when we operated outside of His will and did our own rebellious thing. In fact, after we reflect on the experience of waywardness with the renewed perspective the Holy Spirit gives us in repentance, we will be able to see that God was, in fact, leading us through every detail of the ordeal.

Are you wondering why I said such a thing? Because Jonah's book is masterfully written – replete with statements implying God's sovereignty over him and his ordeal. Remember, Jonah's book is a testimony of his waywardness. He writes it at a later time, in the quietness of moments spent reflecting deeply on God's nature and actions toward him while he was in sin. And it is obvious by the way Jonah writes that he now appreciates (to the level of worshipful admiration) the very Presence that he so energetically fled from earlier in his life.

Notice the subtle literary clues that Jonah used to turn his readers thoughts toward God's sovereign work in his life. He recorded the events of his errant life and God's specific discipline with terms that cannot be misunderstood. He intended for his readers to perfectly perceive that in the midst of his rebellion, God did not abandon him to his state of disobedience, but was present, active, and intimately involved in his life. Hear what he says in his testimony of God's amazingly sovereign work over him,

1:4	*the Lord sent* out a great wind
1:17	*the Lord had prepared* a great fish
2:10	*the Lord spoke* to the fish
4:6	*the Lord God prepared* a plant
4:7	*God prepared* a worm
4:8	*God prepared* a vehement east wind

Look carefully at the consistent refrain of divine elements that were cemented in Jonah's memory of his ordeal. These sovereign-sounding references indicate that Jonah is looking back on his waywardness from a renewed perspective whereby he now understands that God was with him all during his rebellion, as well as bringing about his discipline and orchestrating his restoration.

Reflection focuses our minds on God and His sovereign activity. The lesson inherent in the style in which Jonah wrote grabs me by the lapels and I hope it captures your attention too. Fifty-four times in forty-eight verses God's name or a pronoun substitute is used. This makes it abundantly clear that as Jonah writes, his literary focus is the sovereignty of God over all things. In making this his focus, Jonah wants all his readers to understand that God sovereignly works in men's lives because His mercy and grace is toward sinners (the Ninevites). His mercy and grace is also aimed at erring saints. Contextually, erring saints means *Jonah*, but by way of application it also means *you* and *me*!

We cannot make too much of this. God is God, even in times where we do not recognize His sovereignty over us. When our hearts are not even remotely cognizant of His presence, His commands to us, or His love relationship with us, He is still acting as only He can, as the God who is over all. Repenting and regaining a renewed mind means giving ample consideration to

God's sovereign hand over us amid all of life, and especially the times when our hearts became hard and unresponsive to Him (for whatever reason or in whatever circumstance) and we stumbled in our obedience.

You may need to list the occurrences of your life that you deemed mere coincidence or unpleasant happenstance, then reflect on God's sovereign action during that time. It may surprise you (delightfully so) to be able to see God's hand that led you through those times, even if at the time you went through them, you had no idea He was even there.

Thanksgiving

In 1 Thessalonians 5:18 we are admonished to give thanks in all things. *All things* includes not only the blessings of life, but also (and this is the context of Jonah) the situations of God's discipline where we have come to understand the depth of our wanderings, our heart's tendencies toward hardness and stumbling, and the intimate involvement of God's Spirit to bring us back to spiritual health.

Remember the list in the previous section that you were to make of God's sovereign leading while in your times of wandering? Ask God to help you see that time in your life from His perspective and express your thankfulness for how faithful He was and for how mercifully He cared for you, exercising His benevolent control over your life. God has every right to deal with us according to our sins, but He often extends mercy instead. If we lived through the ordeal of our disobedience, then it is apparent that He mercifully gave more life and care so that we could enter into a deeper understanding of His gracious ways.

Keep expanding your list of God's activity in your life. Keep it in your Bible so that it is near you when you spend time with Him through His Word. Reflect on your Father's goodness as an act of your will, even if your emotions are not on board. Make every effort to focus on God and His involvement with you throughout life. Jonah is our example. This is what he did.

Here's one more thing about thanksgiving. We can never express thankfulness to God while focusing on ourselves or on what God has *not* done. The psalmist said that he would remember all God's benefits (Psalm 103:2). This should be our focus as well. Our sins and failures are many and can easily overwhelm us into permanent ineffectiveness. But the way out of the misery of our failure is to look at God and His faithful work in our lives. His faithfulness will be a fully adequate resource for a grateful heart.

Humility

Refocusing on God involves taking the focus *off* ourselves in recognition of our utter helplessness without Him. While Jonah's book is a writing about himself and his sinful disobedience, it is also one where he skillfully drew the reader's attention to see God *more than* himself. Truly the Chief Actor in this scenario is God on center stage, not Jonah. That is the lesson in our own repentance as well. God is the author of our redemptive relationship. He also is the gracious and sovereign One who leads us into our new-found state of repentance. It is essential to take note of Jonah's humility as we close our study and speak of restoration. For God gives grace to the humble but opposes those who walk in pride (First Peter 5:5). We need God's grace, so we want to learn from Jonah the marks of a humble heart's response to God in discipline.

Honestly, if I were writing this account, I would want to make sure that my audience knew that my heart eventually turned back to the Lord. I would not want my readers left with even the remote possibility of concluding that I never settled my issue with God. I would want them to understand that I came out of it well; I eventually turned. That's the way I would want people to think of me if this were my story.

Not so for Jonah. He did not sense that he should add a fifth chapter to his book, a chapter which recorded his own repentance and restoration. It is obvious to me that he *did* repent and that he *was* restored. He could not have written with such an intense focus on God and His sovereignty while maintaining a distant relationship from God. No, the things Jonah wrote and the way in which he wrote communicate clearly that the relationship he now enjoys with God is indeed a close one. Therefore, I am convinced that Jonah repented and returned to a humble posture of submission to God and an intimate relationship with Him, even though the inspired text does not explicitly say so.

Our sinful flesh needs to be dealt repeated death blows. Even in repentance, we are too often concerned about how we may appear in the eyes of others. But repentance with humility means that when the story of our ordeal is told, we do not sense the necessity to ensure that the story ends with ourselves in a favorable light. Jonah's humility caused him to leave himself in a most *unfavorable* light. And the point is this, if we are genuine in our return to God, like Jonah we ought to be at rest that we are *in God*. Thoughts of ourselves, what others see and conclude about us are all but unimportant when it comes to the matter of our repentance. This is true Christlike humility as revealed to us in Philippians 2:7. Speaking of Jesus in His humiliation and suffering: "but made Himself of no reputation, taking the form of a bond servant." In bringing men to God, Jesus' humility did not take into account His status in the minds of those around Him. Should it not then behoove us as His servants to act accordingly, especially when we are returning to Him in repentance and faith? The reality is that in time our lives will show what has happened within our hearts. Having a restored relationship with God, one where He is worshipped and adored as our Maker, Defender, Redeemer, and Friend (as the old hymn would say it) is all that should matter to us.

Conclusion

What need has God shown you that may be lurking unaddressed or untended in your heart, as evidenced by the level of your obedience to His clearly revealed commands? What issue might there be that has already begun to bring you down and harden your heart toward the lost around you, people to whom God has called you to proclaim His gospel?

Perhaps you are in the depths of despair due to your own sinful choices. *God* and *only God* can heal you. But that healing may only come through the deep, soul-cleansing pain of His discipline, a reminder of His calling upon your life, and a great humbling on your part to embrace what God offers. Only God's Word (the Scriptures) can reveal the deep, dark parts of our hearts. Only His Word can give you the necessary insight concerning your heart and the courage to confront your own need.

What Jeremiah pleaded in prayer to God is the only hope any of us have of being restored: "Heal me, O Lord, and I shall be healed; save me, and I shall be saved" (Jeremiah 17:14). I trust that all who read these words will act on the truths revealed in Jonah's book to find healing for their hearts.

May God, who alone tenaciously pursues sinners in order to restore them, bring you back into a relationship of intimacy with Himself that brings you unending joy and utter delight in Him alone. And may the people in your life who still need Christ hear of Him through you, God's joyfully obedient servant, who has put aside the sins that so easily cause a stumbling toward obedience.

A Final Word

After Jesus had sent out the seventy disciples to preach the gospel, they returned amazed and astounded at the power they experienced, that even demons were subject to them in Jesus' name. Jesus' comment immediately following their remarks are worthy of consideration. Luke 10:18 records His words, "I saw Satan falling from heaven like lightening,"

The vision our Lord saw, along with the proximity of His comments to His disciples' words, make me take serious thought of what is being communicated. We know from the Old Testament that Satan is the accuser of God's people.[14] Both Job and Joshua the High Priest experienced the rancorous accusations of God's arch enemy. The New Testament enlightens us to this reality even further.

> Then I heard a loud voice saying in heaven, "Now salvation, and strength, and the kingdom of our God, and the power of His Christ have come, for the accuser of our brethren, *who accused them before our God day and night,* as been cast down.[15] (emphasis mine)

---

[14] Job 1:6-12; 2:1-7; Zechariah 3:1

[15] Revelation 12:10

Whatever else the words of our Lord mean in Luke 10, it seems apparent that what Jesus saw visualizes for us the disarming effect the proclamation of the gospel has on our chief enemy, Satan. The disciples returned from their short term mission trip and recounted how they saw the demons becoming subject to them. As real as this was, Jesus wanted them to know something else, that their obedience to proclaim the gospel of salvation through Christ alone was the impetus for Satan himself falling from the place where he (with unimaginably pervasive malice and all-encompassing evil) accuses God's people before God's face perpetually. His falling from heaven appears to communicate that he doesn't have an accusing leg to stand on when God's people are engaging God's commands to proclaim the good news of eternal life through Jesus.

If you make the decision to live in consistent obedience to Christ by speaking the truth of the Gospel to those around you, you will be taking the teeth out of the chief accuser's rantings against you. On the other hand, continuing a life of disengagement toward the command of Jesus in the Great Commission is, in effect, allowing your enemy to have the upper hand in your life. This is not the choice that any believer ought to be making.

God's heart from the beginning of time has been for His world. To Abraham, in Genesis 12:2, God said, "In you all the families of the earth shall be blessed." This somewhat cryptic statement at the time was fully unveiled centuries later by the apostle Paul as he wrote,

> And the Scripture, foreseeing that God would justify the Gentiles by faith, preached the gospel to Abraham beforehand, saying, "In you all the nations shall be blessed." So then those who are of faith are blessed with believing Abraham.[16]

---

[16] Galatians 3:8,9

And again,

> And if you are Christ's then you are Abraham's seed, and heirs according to the promise.[17]

What we are doing in New Testament times by proclaiming the gospel of Jesus Christ is in many respects simply continuing what God began in ages past through His promise to Abraham, that which has unfolded throughout the centuries of earth's history.

Repeatedly, God has reminded readers of holy Scripture that His glory will one day completely envelope this planet. Habakkuk 2:14 says, "For the earth will be filled with the knowledge of the glory of the Lord, as the waters cover the sea." That is His plan, that His rightful place of recognition as the authoritative Creator and Father over all. That this would be seen, embraced, and worshipped by all His creation is God's goal.

God's promise that His glory will cover the earth will one day be fulfilled literally, and every person on the planet will recognize His presence and authority. But until then, in this age of grace and gospel proclamation, His glory is being placed within people one soul at a time, as the message of the gospel is given, as it is believed and embraced, and as lives are transformed by the power of the risen Christ.

That God would allow believers who have experienced His life-changing grace to then dispense this grace to others is a blessed calling and the moment you are God's instrument for bringing another soul into His family, you will experience an amazing thrill, that you, a lowly sinner saved by grace, have been privileged to witness His power to save and transform a life. Furthermore, your experience will motivate you to see the transforming power of the gospel more and more. Truly, for the genuine child of God,

---

[17] Galatians 3:29

nothing is more thrilling than being God's instrument for bringing the grace of the gospel's salvation to others, seeing them be born again from darkness to light, from death to life, and from lives that were perpetual blasphemy to lives that give God consistent glory.

God, residing within each of His redeemed ones in the person of His Spirit, reminds us of our calling through His Word and empowers us to engage His agenda for His world. He has spoken, and He is speaking now. God has given us His calling to take the truth of sins perfectly and completely paid for at Calvary to people who are lost and in need of being saved. My prayer for you, fellow follower of Christ, is that you do what God has called you to do.

> God was in Christ reconciling the world to Himself,
> not imputing their trespasses to them,
> and has committed to us the word of reconciliation.
> Now we are ambassadors for Christ, as
> though God were pleading
> through us: we implore you on Christ's
> behalf, be reconciled to God.
>
> —Second Corinthians 5:19,20

Lightning Source UK Ltd.
Milton Keynes UK
UKHW010130150223
416983UK00001B/310

9 781449 799076